Endorsements

I think being a student pastor is one of the hardest jobs on the planet. That's why I'm thrilled that folks like my friends Ben and Kevin are addressing the unique challenges of student ministry with a fresh perspective. And best of all, they don't pull any punches—refer to the chapter titles if you have any doubts. As a dad with daughters headed toward adolescence I'm deeply encouraged that resources like *Make Believe* are going to dramatically amplify the critical work student pastors do.

JON ACUFF, NEW YORK TIMES BESTSELLING AUTHOR OF *START* AND *STUFF CHRISTIANS LIKE*

Make Believe takes a practical approach to some uncommon principles that can make or break your ministry. Crawshaw and Ragsdale invite you to imagine again and equip you to continue dreaming.

MARK MATLOCK, EXECUTIVE DIRECTOR, YOUTH SPECIALTIES

After 30+ years in student ministry, I'm more convinced than ever that our niche of ministry is one of the most difficult and important jobs in the church. That's why I'm so grateful that Ben and Kevin have written a resource that not only encourages student pastors to stay the course, but gives them some practical tips to effectively take their ministry to the next level. This isn't just theory. *Make Believe* offers doable strategies from real leaders in real churches. To remain relevant and engaging to teenagers over the span of one's career will require us to re-imagine the way we do ministry over and over. And that is what *Make Believe* invites us to do: Re-imagine our strategy. Re-imagine our role. Re-imagine our relationships with students, parents, and even our own church staff.

DOUG FIELDS, AUTHOR OF THE BEST-SELLING *PURPOSE-DRIVEN YOUTH MINISTRY, YOUR FIRST TWO YEARS IN YOUTH MINISTRY*, AND CO-FOUNDER OF DOWNLOADYOUTHMINISTRY.COM.

Some days youth ministry leaves you asking, "what is the point, exactly"? Some days you might feel like an event planner, game creator, camp fundraiser, announcement giver, safety inspector, liability detective, official notary, financial manager, media developer, or first-responder. But there is so much more to be discovered and offered in youth ministry than the functional hats we wear. Ben and Kevin know this firsthand. They know there are days when the gritty and sometimes overwhelming reality of our roles beg us to reimagine them, our relationships, and the "why" behind the "what" we do week after week. This is the type of conversation that every youth ministry leader should be having with someone. And this book is a great place to start.

BROOKLYN LINDSEY, AUTHOR, SPEAKER, AND YOUTH PASTOR AT HIGHLAND PARK CHURCH IN LAKELAND, FLORIDA

I have witnessed the imagination and genius leadership of Ben Crawshaw and Kevin Ragsdale first-hand. The powerfully simple and practical principles that shape *Make Believe* are not just philosophical fluff. They are real, timeless, and proven. Ben and Kevin are humble, honest, unassuming leaders. *Make Believe* sends a timely and important reminder that, as youth leaders, "Tomorrow will look a whole lot like today unless you learn to lead with some imagination." I needed this book. I love this book. You will too.

STUART HALL, ORANGE LEADER, COMMUNICATOR, CO-AUTHOR OF *THE SEVEN CHECKPOINTS* AND *MAX Q*

MAKE BELIEVE

Published by Orange
a division of The reThink Group, Inc.
5870 Charlotte Lane, Suite 300
Cumming, GA 30040 U.S.A.

All Scripture quotations, unless otherwise noted, are taken from *The Holy Bible, New International Version*®, *NIV*® Copyright © 1973, 1978, 1984, 2011 by Biblica, Inc.® Used by permission. All rights reserved worldwide. Other Orange products are available online and direct from the publisher.

Visit www.OrangeBooks.com and www.ThinkOrange.com for more resources like these.

ISBN: 978-1-941259-04-7

©2014 Ben Crawshaw and Kevin Ragsdale

Writers: Ben Crawshaw, Kevin Ragsdale
Lead Editor: Crystal Chiang
Editorial Team: Holly Crawshaw, Kristen Ivy,
Tim Walker, Natalie White
Art Direction: Ryan Boon
Design: FiveStone

Printed in the United States of America
First Edition 2014

1 2 3 4 5 6 7 8 9 10

04/18/2014

orange

Make Believe

5 things great student pastors choose to believe

BEN CRAWSHAW & KEVIN RAGSDALE

Table of Contents

PART ONE: **GREAT LEADERS MAKE BELIEVE**
10 .... Head In The Clouds
14 .... The Spark
17 .... Catalysts For Change

PART TWO: **YOU WILL BE HERE FOREVER**
22 .... Highs And Lows
24 .... The Most Important Job In The World
28 .... Reverse The Turnover Rate
31 .... The Training Ground
36 .... *One:*   *Work On Making It Great*
39 .... *Two:*   *Build A Network*
42 .... *Three:*   *Develop A Strategy*
44 .... *Four:*   *Never Stop Learning*

PART THREE: **YOU WILL LEAVE ONE DAY**
50 .... The Problem With Doing It All
52 .... The Rock Star Mentality
54 .... Build A Bigger Base
58 .... *One:*   *Re-Prioritize Your Time*
61 .... *Two:*   *Share The Spotlight*
63 .... *Three:*   *Check Your Ego*

PART FOUR: **YOUR SENIOR PASTOR IS RIGHT**
70 .... Who's Responsible?
72 .... Follow The Leader
75 .... Walk In His Shoes
78 .... Live What You Want Them To Learn
80 .... *One:*   *Ask The Question*
82 .... *Two:*   *The 40-List*
83 .... *Three:*   *Learn Something Together*
84 .... *Four:*   *Follow*

PART FIVE: **YOUR CHILDREN'S PASTOR IS COOL**

88 .... Children's Pastors Have A Tough Job

90 .... The Importance Of Childhood

92 .... Serve Or Be Served

94 .... Benefits Of Working Together

97 .... *One:*   *Connect As Human Beings*

98 .... *Two:*   *Work On Something Together*

99 .... *Three:*   *Make Kids Heroes In Your Student Ministry*

100 .... *Four:*   *Serve Your Children's Pastor*

PART SIX: **YOU NEED PARENTS**

106 .... Exceptions To The Rule

108 .... Lasting Influence

110 .... Speaking "Family"

112 .... The Need To Be Needed

115 .... *One:*   *Connect Parents With Leaders*

117 .... *Two:*   *Connect Parents With Your Strategy*

119 .... *Three:*   *Connect Parents With Other Parents*

120 .... *Four:*   *Connect Parents With Their Kids*

122 .... *Five:*   *Connect Parents With Big Moments*

PART SEVEN: **IT STARTS WITH YOU**

128 .... The Next Generation

GREAT LEADERS MAKE BELIEVE

Head In The Clouds

I (Ben) remember it vividly. Me, nine years old, playing basketball in my driveway.

I grew up in the pre-subdivision days, when having land was king. The neighbors I played with were within biking—not walking—distance, so it wasn't always possible to coordinate hangout time. My closest sibling, my sister, was five years older and much more interested in Finger Pop Mittens and Madonna's "Lucky Star" than she was shooting hoops with me. My dad was at work.

Needless to say, I was ballin' solo that day.

It was the golden era for my hometown Atlanta Hawks: Dominique Wilkins, Spud Webb, and Doc Rivers. We even had a center named Tree Rollins. How can you not love an NBA team with a Spud, a Doc, and a Tree?

The '85-'86 Hawks finished first in the NBA Central Division that season. And the icing on the cake? Dominique won the Slam Dunk Contest in '85; Spud Webb won it in '86. I was captivated by our high-flyers.

So I would imagine that I was the Hawks' starting point guard (sorry Doc Rivers). And not just the point guard, I was the unquestioned physical and emotional leader of the team. I'd have pretend conversations with Dominique during pretend timeouts. I'd direct traffic on the court. It was a great time!

Inevitably, we'd end up in the NBA Finals matched up against the Lakers. It was a highly publicized duel between Magic Johnson and me. It would always come down to game seven. It would always come down to the last shot.

And I would always take it.

Most of the time I missed that shot because I was a terrible shooter. This allowed for some solid chronokinesis. For those of you who are rusty on your superpower lingo, that's time travel. I would basically run the play over and over until I *finally* made the shot. The crowd would go wild. I'm talking out-of-control crazy. The Hawks won the NBA Finals! It was unanimous—I was the Finals' MVP.

I was just about to answer Pat O'Brien's first post-game interview question when my mom called me inside for dinner. Just like that I went from one of the greatest basketball players in the world to a fourth grader who didn't want to eat meatloaf.

Imagination time over. Back to reality.

But for an hour or two, it was magical. I was a world-class athlete at age nine. How cool is that? All the realistic obstacles were gone—my age and lack of actual basketball ability. I was the best version of myself. I was on top of the NBA world.

Do you remember playing make believe as a kid? Some of you were probably too logical and mature. But I bet most of you had *something* that you pretended to be. A superhero? A princess? An astronaut? Make believe doesn't always have to be epic. My wife would make believe that she was a grocery store cashier.

Since the beginning of time, boys and girls have been storming castles, catching bad guys, fighting fires, and searching for hidden treasure (I'm not sure if they have actually been doing it since the beginning of time, but it seemed like a cool way to start that sentence). But here's the problem:

 IMAGINATION IS HIGHLY SUPPORTED IN CHILDHOOD, BUT IT'S HIGHLY SUPPRESSED IN ADULTHOOD.

Eventually, we lose the ability to make believe. As we grow up, we're told to "get our head out of the clouds" and "use our brains." But isn't imagination the very thing that has catapulted us to do great things? It's put humans in the air, under the sea, and on the moon. If you drive to work, you're benefitting from someone's imagination. If you ride the train, you're benefitting, too. If you check your email on your phone while you wait for your stop . . . well, you get the idea.

When you think about it, imagination and faith are similar. They both stir us to believe something or believe *in* someone. That's why anti-faith people use the same language that anti-imagination people use: "Get your head out of the clouds" and "use your brain."

But you and I were created in the *image* of God. I'm not sure I know exactly what that means, but I think part of that "image" shows up in our imagination. Think about it. Human beings are the only species with the ability to imagine what doesn't exist and create it. As great as pets are, I doubt you've ever had one who pretended to be a robot and then made a robot friend out of cardboard and dryer vents.

$\longrightarrow$ **FAITH TAKES IMAGINATION.**

I'm not saying faith is only imagination. But you need a little imagination if you're going to envision a God you can't see or pray to —a God you can't hear audibly.

Just like it's sad when a kid has reached the age when he or she is too old to play make believe—when they become too aware of their obstacles and the worst version of themselves—it's sad when we as adults quit imagining how things *could* be, and what it might take to get us there. We let real life keep us from believing that there could be a better way. In other words, **we let the harshness of reality weaken the hope of our faith.**

Now, let's turn all of that to you and your role in student ministry.

- Are you imagining?
- Are you dreaming?
- Is your faith growing?
- Or have you let reality stifle your ability to believe?

I hope this book builds your faith. And I hope it catapults you to imagine a better way to lead students.

When you're a leader, you have influence. Whether you believe that or not, it's true. And when you use your imagination, it gives those who follow you permission to do the same. Sometimes people use the phrase "cast vision." That's a fancy way of saying that you paint a picture that other people can imagine and give them a vision of something they can believe in. Actually, it's much quicker and easier to say "cast vision," so just stick with that.

When you seek to inspire people, you're attempting to say or do something that helps others build their belief.

Think of it this way:

LEADERSHIP $\longrightarrow$ **IMAGINATION** $\longrightarrow$ **BELIEF**

Steve Jobs was a modern technology prophet. As the co-founder of consumer electronics powerhouse Apple, Jobs didn't just lead the charge—he *was* the charge in revolutionizing the computer industry. Whether you're an Apple lover or hater, you can't argue with the company's ability to innovate. Jobs built a loyal and passionate customer-base that deeply believes in the products Apple creates.

It was Jobs' dream to inspire users with a unique electronic experience that they could easily navigate. In Carmine Gallo's book *The Innovation Secrets of Steve Jobs: Insanely Different Principles for Breakthrough Success,* he notes that Jobs believed **innovation distinguishes between a leader and a follower.**

Jobs never lost his ability to imagine. Instead, he used his imagination to innovate. And with that innovation, Jobs inspired people to believe in him as a leader. The result? Astonishing momentum. If you own an iPhone, iPad, iMac, or any of the many Apple products, then you believe in the imagination of Steve Jobs. You are following his leadership.

Nelson Mandela was also a man with a relentless vision. His determination to end racial discrimination in South Africa earned him 27 years in prison. Quite a different payoff than Jobs, who got a billion-dollar company. Yet, despite his imprisonment, Mandela never stopped pushing people toward equality and reform. Mandela imagined a different South Africa and invited the South African people to imagine it with him. He saw hope, restoration, and freedom instead of poverty, oppression, and hate. He famously put it this way:

"The power of imagination created the illusion that my vision went much farther than the naked eye could actually see." [1]

Mandela led by helping people envision a better country to live in. His imagination helped other people imagine. And their collective imagination, along with a whole lot of determination and effort, literally changed the reality for a whole nation.

In Galilee, when Jesus told His followers, *"Go and make disciples of all nations,"* [2] He helped them imagine a movement that would take His message to Jews and Gentiles around the world. And when He added, *"And surely I am with you always, to the very end of the age,"* [3] He instilled belief that it was actually possible.

Then Jesus left. What happens next is the book of Acts. Talk about people who could've been overwhelmed by the harsh reality of their circumstances! Instead, a band of unlikely trailblazers, led by Peter and filled with the Holy Sprit, established the irresistible movement of the church.

Decades later, when Peter wrote to a group of Christians in Asia Minor, he said, *"To those who through the righteousness of our God and Savior Jesus Christ have received a faith as precious as ours..."* [4]

Wait. A faith as precious as the Apostles'? A faith as precious as the missionaries' who put their lives at risk? A faith as precious as Peter's? Yes. Peter was letting them know that he didn't have some elusive, superior faith because he was one of the church's founding fathers. No, *everyone* had access to a faith that was just "as precious."

Peter gave these early Christians something to believe in. Shortly afterward, he was martyred. But the movement continued.

Leaders use their imagination to spark faith in others. Leaders invite people to believe in something they may not otherwise believe in—something that feels unlikely or unattainable. Jobs did it. Mandela did it. Peter did it. Jesus did it.

Now you go do it.

As leaders who lead students, think about this: it's impossible to improve something without imagination. You can't change something without imagining something better. **Your tomorrow will look a whole lot like today unless you learn to lead with some imagination.**

So you *must* imagine! Make believe is essential to your leadership and their faith.

Catalysts For Change

Growing up in Oklahoma City, I (Kevin) loved going to my church. And I was unembarrassed to be vocal about it. In high school when my friends stayed at my house on Saturday nights, they had no choice but to tag along with me to church on Sunday mornings. I thought it was a perfect finish to a great weekend.

Then my friends quit staying at my house on Saturday nights.

Looking back, I realize that I went to church because I believed it was the best place on Earth to be. I thought church was fun and engaging. My friends, however, had a different set of beliefs. They thought church was boring and weird.

I thought the problem was that my friends didn't have enough conviction or devotion to God. In reality, they just had different thoughts about church. And honestly, my church could've done some things to make the experience more appealing for them. (They were invited to join the Handbell Choir. What more did they want?) In the end, I showed up at church because I believed it was great. They avoided church because they believed it was bad.

It's a small example of a powerful idea: if you can change the way you think, you're on your way to changing the way you act. Paul said it this way: *"Be transformed by the renewing of your mind."*[5] You'll see a change in behavior once you imagine a change in belief.

 You can create change not only by doing something differently, but also by believing differently.

There's a relationship between what you believe and what you do that's important to understand. It's the reason why, if you communicate to students, you don't simply say "do this" or "stop doing that" and then close in prayer. Instead, you clearly explain the *why*, because you want to change their belief—not just their behavior—in order to shape their future.

The purpose of this book is to offer five specific things that we want you to believe. But we won't stop there. In the second half of each section, we're going to provide some specific behaviors that will help reinforce that belief. Why? Because we're confident of this:

IMAGINATION + BEHAVIOR = BELIEF

We want you to imagine what your student ministry could look like. And we want you to develop some behaviors that could make that dream a reality.

Imagine it. Do it. And in the end, we hope you believe it.

Let's practice a little make believe, shall we?

If you could make believe that you were any famous person in the world right now, who would you be?

Back to reality. What is the best version of you as a ministry leader?

What is the best version of your student ministry?

If you could change one thing about your student ministry, what would it be?

YOU WILL
BE HERE
FOREVER

Highs And Lows

Any time you have doubts about God's faithfulness, just re-read the story of Joseph in the book of Genesis. If you're not familiar with the story, put this book down and go check it out. Start in Genesis 37. You'll get a lot more out of that story than you will this book.

Talk about a physical, mental, spiritual, and emotional roller coaster! Minus the imprisonment, slavery, and life-in-danger moments, it's a lot like student ministry. Okay, that may be a stretch. But Joseph's life points *straight* to the loyalty of God. And, it's enough to bring a tear to your eye.

Think about the craziness of Joseph's life:

HIGHS:

1. He had a great relationship with his dad.
2. He had dreams that were actually divine revelations from God.
3. He earned the favor of Potiphar.
4. He earned the favor of the prison warden.
5. He was elevated to second in command by Pharaoh.
6. He saved an entire country.
7. He saved the lives of his family members.

LOWS:

1. His brothers were jealous of him.
2. His brothers plotted to murder him.
3. His brothers sold him into slavery for less than $500 dollars.
4. He was falsely accused of rape.
5. He was unfairly thrown into prison.
6. He was forgotten by the cupbearer for two years.
7. He was separated from his family for over twenty years.

We don't mean to weaken the story by putting it in numbered bullet points (at least it's a list of seven, the holy number). We just wanted to give you a snapshot of what Joseph went through.

But here's why Joseph is so amazing: he remained strong. He kept going. He was a rock, both in spirit and in character. He didn't whine and complain his way through life's ups and downs. He didn't throw in the towel to temptation. And every low point he faced provided an opportunity for God's grace to move in Joseph's life.

If you are a student pastor, here is the biblical word we want you to grab ahold of: **PERSEVERANCE.**

Student ministry isn't easy. (Hopefully no one sold you that lie.) It has its own list of lows. Some of them will be unique to your situation, and some of them simply come with the profession.

You don't know what God is up to *right now* in your life. And you don't know what God is up to in the lives of your students. If you compare *complaining about your job* and *trusting in God's faithfulness* on a scale, where do you sit? If you put *looking for a way out* and *looking for a way to grow*, where are you?

We want to encourage you to build your faith muscle. If you have to, make believe that perseverance is strong in your spirit and character.

And then keep going!

The Most Important Job In The World

Middle and high school span seven years, but their impact lasts forever. Adolescence is an important time—arguably the *most* important. So here's a question for you: **Why would you want to be anywhere else?** There's no other job more needed than the one you're doing right now. Don't let anybody tell you otherwise.

Jennifer Senior (yes, that's her name) wrote an incredible article in *New York Magazine* titled, "Why You Never Truly Leave High School." In it she quotes numerous scholars who've done extensive research in the field of adolescence. She cites one psychologist who highlights the developmental difference between childhood and the teenage years:

> *"If you're interested in making sure kids learn a lot in school, yes, intervening in early childhood is the time to do it," says Laurence Steinberg, a developmental psychologist at Temple University and perhaps the country's foremost researcher on adolescence. "But if you're interested in how people become who they are, so much is going on in the adolescent years."* [1]

Senior goes on to talk about how, at a time when teenagers are 'becoming who they are,' they're bombarded with adversity:

> *"For many people, that's the high-school experience in a nutshell. At the time they experience the most social fear, they have the least control; at the time they're most sensitive to the impressions of others, they're plunked into an environment where it's treacherously easy to be labeled and stuck on a shelf. 'Shame,'" says Brené Brown, a researcher at the University of Houston, "is*

all about unwanted identities and labels. And I would say that for 90 percent of the men and women I've interviewed, their unwanted identities and labels started during their tweens and teens."

Wow. These are the students we get access to week after week. And they need us—the church.

But just because they need us doesn't mean they'll show up. There's no shortage of stuff fighting and competing to grab their attention—stuff that has the potential to quickly make church seem boring.

And then they get their driver's licenses, right? All of a sudden, they have the freedom to go where they want, when they want. This is when a lot of students fade from church. Not to be pessimistic, but think about it: they are often *one* dating relationship, *one* weekend party, or *one* anti-church conversation away from drifting into oblivion. Keeping students engaged is no easy task, which makes leadership during this critical time all that much more important. It's enough to make your blood pressure rise as a student pastor.

But before we get to the good news, we have more bad news to talk about. Did you know . . .

- **In 2014, according to the American Psychological Association, teens reported higher stress levels than adults for the first time ever** [2]
- **1 in 9 students will attempt suicide before their senior year** [3]
- **1 out of every 200 girls between the ages of 13 and 19 cut themselves on a regular basis** [4]
- **30% of U.S. students in grades six through ten are involved in moderate or frequent bullying—as bullies, as victims, or as both** [5]

It hurts, doesn't it?

Now think about this—in addition to living in a society where the above statistics exist, teenagers are simultaneously grappling with complications that are inherent to their season of life. As a starting point, let's talk about three of them.

1. **RELATIONSHIPS**

   Most students don't go to prom because they love to dance. They don't go to Starbucks because they love coffee. They don't even go to high school football games because they love football. (Most of the students who love football are playing.) They go *because their friends are there.*

   When I (Ben) was in high school, a group of us would go to a nearby gas station after school. Most towns have *that* gas station. Because of my family's financial situation, I rarely had extra money. So I only walked inside a couple of times. My mid-90's gas station snacks of choice, by the way, were either Mountain Dew and Fun Dip, or Mountain Dew and Funyuns. (I was hyper-committed to fun.) We didn't get gas. We didn't do *anything* except shoot the breeze, even though we had just spent an entire day together at school.

   Students have an insatiable appetite for relationships. An adult may want to go somewhere and be an anonymous face in the crowd, but most students don't want that. They want to *belong.* Student ministry is perfectly positioned to provide that—to not only capture students' need for interaction, but also to reach their hearts. It's like the gas station, hopefully cleaner.

2. **MEMORIES**

   Think about all the unforgettable moments that student ministry can create. Some of those moments are deeply spiritual and emotional and will forever shape the future of a teenager. Some of those moments are shallow, random, and ridiculous. But they, too, will forever be great memories. I love the fact that both of them are connected to the Church.

3. **FAITH**

   Most of us would agree that the teenage years represent the era when students begin creating space between their parents and them.

It makes sense for a 13-year-old to have more freedom than a 6-year-old. And it makes sense for a 17-year-old to have more freedom than a 13-year-old.

In the midst of that growing freedom, it's crucial for students to begin owning their faith. Emotionally and intellectually grasping it outside of their parents' faith.

Don't you love it when middle school students have eye-opening moments? When they *experience* some of the things they've heard? Don't you love it when high school students ask difficult questions? Even if you don't have the answers, it's awesome to begin the dialogue and the journey for answers. Don't you love it when teenagers see that there's a bigger "Church"—and a bigger mission—than what they experience within your four walls once or twice a week?

Now imagine *that* time period without student ministry?

Imagine that time period with *bad* student ministry?

Reverse The Turnover Rate

The other day I (Kevin) was looking through student ministry stuff on the Internet. If you want to be gracious, call it 'research.' I came across a website that talked about student pastors' obstacles to hanging in there longer than three years. Lack of training and appreciation, unrealistic expectations, and burnout were some of the main culprits. The writer explained how one student pastor, out of sheer survival, stayed in his first student ministry job for six years:

> *"Time became the most effective teacher. [He] learned that the longer he stayed at a church, the greater the trust. And the greater the trust, the more teenagers were able to clearly articulate their values and beliefs before they moved into adulthood."* [6]

We've been hard-pressed to find statistics that reveal the *actual* turnover rate in student ministry. Perhaps it's difficult because many student pastors are part-time or work multiple jobs within the church. But we do know this: we've yet to see *any* data that reveals an average tenure of four years or longer. So to be super conservative and wildly unscientific, here's our stat:

STUDENT PASTOR TENURE < **FOUR YEARS**

Ironically, that's similar to the average playing career of an NFL football player. So in that sense, you're not in bad company! But outside of that, student ministers don't have a great track record of longevity. Talking to senior pastors and executive pastors around the country, it's surprising how many of them seem to imply, *I don't expect him or her to be around too much longer.* The deeper implication is, *I've seen it time and time again.*

If you're like us, you're probably not okay with other student pastors giving this profession a bad reputation. Does the church-world see us as quitters?

When we were engaged, Holly and I (Ben) got the same advice lots of couples get: *Don't let divorce be an option when you get married.* One lady told us to never mention the word or even let the thought enter our minds. That seems a bit extreme, but I see the point: it's not beneficial to view it as a potential escape. This is not a book on marriage, by the way.

Fortunately my wife has never done something so terrible that I've had to remind myself of that advice. I, on the other hand, have probably done a thing or two. But I'll save that for another book. (Maybe an autobiography that only my mom will read?)

But when you believe you'll be here forever—when you approach your job with absolute commitment—it gives you some unique tools.

CONFIDENCE	**VISION**	**CONTENTMENT**
You tackle difficult topics head-on because you know that you will be the one to deal with the consequences of unresolved issues.	You dream of what can be, and you begin to implement changes that will inevitably take longer than two or three years to realize.	It's comforting (and stabilizing) to know that you've put a period at the end of your professional sentence. Not a comma or an ellipses—a period.

I could name a few more, but you get the idea.

Imagine if you put a period at the end of it instead of an ellipsis.

I AM A STUDENT PASTOR.

vs

I AM A STUDENT PASTOR . . .

You already know teenagers are affected when there's instability in their home. You work with them, so you see the effects regularly: one day dad is in the house, the next day he's out.

What about the turnover rate in student ministry? Doesn't that hurt, too? It doesn't hurt to the same degree as uncertainty at home, but it still has a negative effect. Teenagers need predictability, and they deserve someone who will stay committed to them longer than it takes to finish their Kaplan course.

Like a college student returning home for Christmas break to a stable household, we *love* the idea of your former students knowing that you're still in the game—staying faithful and passionate—and that they can come back and see you anytime.

The Training Ground

One of my countless "flop" moments in student ministry came one Sunday night when I (Ben) planned a Fiesta-themed party. I called it an "outreach night," which simply translated to "Relax outside world, there won't be any preacher time." So off I went, planning a night that would compel scores of unchurched students to forever fall in love with church.

Games. Flop.

Funny videos. Flop. No one laughed except the three of us who made them.

As part of my grand scheme to elevate the Fiesta theme, our staff ordered a throng of Taco Bell soft tacos to be available for the reaping at the end of the night.

Budget. Flop. As cheap as Taco Bell is, ordering enough of *anything* gets expensive.

Don't get me wrong, students *loved* eating them. And throwing them. And stepping on them. And doing whatever it is that students do with Taco Bell.

Clean student room. Flop.

When the night was over, no one had to tell me, "You know Ben, I just don't think tonight was a success." I knew it. It was terrible.

As I crawled on the floor, cleaning smeared taco-ness out of the carpet, this question ran through my mind: *What in the world am I doing?* The same question haunted me as I drove home. And for about two weeks after.

Have you ever asked that? Have you ever been in the middle of . . .
   buying supplies for games,
   reprimanding eager teenage boys for being too "touchy",
   breaking up a social media war between two sophomore girls,

. . . and asked yourself, *What is the point?*

Sometimes it's hard to find significance in your right-now job. And maybe you can't wait until you move on to what's next—when you can work with people who don't throw things at people while you're speaking.

Hey, we're not criticizing the idea of training in student ministry until you get more experience and seasoning under your belt. Maybe you do have visions of being a senior pastor one day. But we would suggest thinking of your job this way:

 A TRAINING GROUND > **A STEPPING STONE**

If you are planning on doing something different later, doesn't that make your work all that much more important now? Wouldn't that lead you to think, *Man, I better be a great steward of this time to prepare me for what's next?* Give it all you've got right now. Learn everything you can in this season.

Don't just build your resume, build your faith. It's so inspiring the way Paul challenges us, *"Whatever you do, work at it with all your heart, as working for the Lord, not for human masters,"* (Colossians *3:23*). You should give this every bit of your passion and energy, even if you're buying 50 crickets from the pet store to play Cricket Spit (we don't recommend it). Under no circumstances should you become an unhealthy workaholic, but you should constantly check yourself to see if you're doing this with all your heart.

By the way, there's a comma at the end of that verse. Paul continues, *". . .since you know that you will receive an inheritance from the Lord as a reward. It is the Lord Christ you are serving."* Wow, *that's* a convicting verse! This idea is more about your faith than it is your job description.

Here's our opinion—feel free to take it or leave it: **If you view student ministry as a stepping stone, that's exactly what you're going to do—step on it.** Landscapers don't nurture and cultivate steppingstones like they do flowerbeds. They simply install them so they can walk on them to get where they're going.

Ministry isn't a corporate ladder. It's a calling. We're not saying that you won't—or shouldn't—do something different one day. We're just saying that you ought to try staying fully enthralled in what you're doing *now* until God calls you to do something else *later.*

WHEN YOU
MAKE BELIEVE
YOU'LL
BE HERE
FOREVER . . .

1. You develop perseverance.

2. You gain more confidence and contentment.

3. You foster a vision for your ministry that's bigger than the next six months.

4. You have a greater impact on the students you serve.

5. You grow leadership skills that will help you prepare for what's next.

For some of you, the reason you're not the superhero version of yourself as a student pastor is because you've never viewed student ministry as a job to be a superhero in. You've viewed it as a job to practice doing ministry until you get a "real" church job.

With all of that being said, we want to give you four things you can start doing now that will put some legs on your faith.

IF YOU MAKE BELIEVE THAT YOU'LL BE HERE FOREVER, YOU WILL . . .

ONE: WORK ON MAKING IT GREAT

When I (Ben) was 28 years old, I took a new job in student ministry at North Point Community Church. At the time, North Point's *staff* was twice the size of my previous church's (North Georgia Bible Chapel) entire congregation. To this day, I'm not sure I've ever prayed about something as much as I prayed about whether or not I should make that move.

When I finally pulled the trigger, I was in a transition tornado: I had just married the love of my life, just built a new house, and now I had a new job. Oh yeah, I was also adjusting to a new church (and church staff) culture. Talk about a deer in the headlights!

There are pros and cons of big churches and small churches. After working for six years at a church of 150, and six years at a church of over 15,000, I love them both. Neither are perfect, but both are effective.

As I was settling in to my new role, I scheduled lots of breakfasts and lunches with other staff members. North Point has a bunch of smart folks running around that place.

I hope I'm not exaggerating here (although I may be): in two weeks, six different men asked me this question:

 "WHERE DO YOU SEE YOURSELF IN FIVE YEARS?"

My mind went into hydromatic (I'm not even sure if that's a word) to figure out the answer to that question. I took personality tests, wrote down life goals, met with a career counselor, and read a stack of books. There's nothing wrong with any of that, but I have a tendency to take new mental ventures over the top.

In the midst of my quest for future clarity—about eight months after I started at North Point—I heard about a job opening in our children's ministry at a different campus. All I knew was it had the word

"Director" in the title. Without talking to my boss, Kevin, I reached out about the job. I got a favorable response. The man I talked to called Kevin that night and asked for permission to interview me.

The next day Kevin and I were driving back to the church after lunch.

Kevin: *"Did you reach out about that director position?"*

Me: *(Uh oh). "Yes."*

Kevin: *"Are you frustrated in your current job?"*

Me: *"No."*

Kevin: *"Then why did you reach out about a different job?"*

I talked for the next fifteen minutes. Let's be real—I verbally vomited. Kevin patiently listened. I can't articulate what I said because it probably didn't make much sense. I talked about things like:

- My future.
- Money.
- Guys who were getting opportunities that I thought I deserved.
- My career path.
- Trying to discover what I was most gifted at.
- My haircut.
- Whether or not I was too old to wear skinny jeans.

It was one of those moments (rare for a male) when you know you should stop talking but you don't. At one point I found myself mentioning names of guys I was jealous of—who does that? To be honest, stepping into a big pond like North Point exposed *a lot* of my insecurities. I'm grateful that I learned about them when I did.

My rant: fifteen minutes. Kevin's response: two minutes. I don't remember *exactly* what he said (probably because I was simultaneously paranoid about what *I* had just said), but this is a summary of what I heard:

 BECOME GREAT AT WHAT YOU'RE DOING *RIGHT NOW,* AND THE FUTURE WILL TAKE CARE OF ITSELF.

That was the last time I ever called about another job.

I put down the career guidance books and went to work on becoming better at what Kevin hired me—and God called me—to do. I'm grateful to Kevin—and more than that, grateful to God—for the opportunities I have *now* because I didn't bail *then*.

TWO: BUILD A NETWORK

When it comes to building a network of fellow student pastors, there are really only two hurdles to jump: jealousy and competition. You don't have to be convinced of how rampant those two things are. **If you can't get to a place in life where you want what's best for other churches, other students, and other leaders, you're in trouble.** If you have to be the top dog in every room you enter, you're in *major* trouble.

We love the following verse because it's so impeccably straightforward and clear:

"As iron sharpens iron, so one person sharpens another."
(Proverbs 27:17)

Nine words: a principle *and* a visual illustration. Ridiculous!

If the verse said, "As iron sharpens nickel, so one person sharpens a different person," that would be a little more confusing. You'd have to figure out which person represents which element of the Earth's outer core.

But it doesn't say that. Instead, it emphasizes the value of having two like-minded people spurring each other on. With that being said, we cannot overstress the importance of having friends who are in the same field. People who . . .
Love students.
Want to engage students with clear, effective, creative, and authentic programming.
Want to do God-honoring, Jesus-centered, Spirit-led student ministry.
Don't want to quit.

As a student pastor, I (Kevin) am always looking for iron. I don't want to over-dramatize or oversell this idea. It's not like we meet once a week and share life-shattering student ministry concepts with each other. But we do meet consistently, and we do learn from each other.

We encourage each other. We steal ideas. We borrow content. We brainstorm solutions to problems.

I think you need some iron in your professional life.

Right now, I can think of 4-5 student pastors around the country who are doing a great job of this. Not because they have *so many* people in their network, but because they're doing such amazing things with their small network. They *lean in* to people in the same field. **They connect instead of *compete.***

In addition to idea-sharing, brainstorming, and encouragement, here are a few other perks:

- **Events.** In the last month, I (Ben) have seen two situations where multiple student ministries have united to go to an event. One was for a ski retreat, and the other was joint registration for summer camp. The benefit for students: more people to get a crush on. The benefit for student pastors: budget reductions. Think about it.

  > Split cost on travel = A happier budget

  Two weeks ago I spoke at a winter retreat that was birthed out of a network. Two of the student pastors went to college together. Three or four smaller churches in the area joined the party. The alignment was impressive.

- **Contacts.** We all know it's way easier to pull off basically *anything* when you have the right people. I (Kevin) can't even count the number of events we did at North Point that were catered by a guy named Hall Veneer. He *loves* to cook, and he loves students. In my early student ministry days, I worked on Hall's landscaping crew. That contact was in the bag!

When I (Ben) was at North Georgia Bible Chapel, I pulled off a lot of crazy videos and sketches for free. There was a lady in our church,

Linda Towns, who was a costume wizard. As we speak, her daughter Tiffany (a former member of the student ministry) is an assistant professor in the Lycoming College theatre department. My brother-in-law, Steve Thomason, owns a video production company, and one of his employees, Ben Grant, was our worship leader. It wasn't my talent—it was my contacts.

I've had conversations that have gone like this:

"Hey, I want to open Sunday night with a rap song, but I don't know anyone who's great at that."

"Bro, I know the *perfect* guy (or girl). They're incredible. I'll send you a YouTube link and their cell phone number. They would *love* the opportunity to perform at more places and get their name out. And they'll do it for free."

I've seen Kevin find great communicators and worship leaders, and it had nothing to do with him flashing the North Point name around. Half of these people had no context for North Point. He found them through his network of student pastors.

In the end, it's just great to *not* work on an island. It's so good for you to know people who do what you do. But not just as passing acquaintances, as friends. It keeps you energized.

You don't have to acquire a huge network. But you need a close one.

THREE: DEVELOP A STRATEGY

What's your strategy?

Seriously, what game plan will you need to be successful in your role as student pastor? When you took this job, you surely hoped to be pretty good at it. So, how do you plan on doing that? Maybe you'd answer with statements like this:

- "I want to make a difference in teenagers' lives."
- "I want to show students the love of Christ."
- "I want to offer something better than what the world offers."
- "I want to train students to live a godly life."

On and on we could go, with incredible statements from good hearts. But the problem is they're not strategies—they're goals. Callings. Promptings. Passions. We know a lot of student pastors who quit student ministry. They had all the passion in the world, but couldn't figure out how to utilize and execute that passion. So they got frustrated or burned-out: lots of hard work, but very little results.

What is it that you want to do? How are you going to accomplish it? Where do you want your student ministry to go? What road are you going to take to get there? Take some time. Go for a drive. Think about it. Pray. Pray some more. Take your staff (if you have one) to a remote cabin and talk it over. There are so many student pastors who never establish—or even think about—a strategy. Don't be in that category.

1. **LOOK IN THE MIRROR.**
   Assess your strengths and weaknesses as a leader. Determine where *you* add the most value and where you need other leaders. Outside of walking step-in-step with the Holy Spirit, there may be no skill greater than emotional intelligence. Are you self-aware? Are you in tune with what it's like to be around you? Or are you doing things that you have no business doing?

Do you have people who are speaking into you as a student pastor? Are you growing as a person and as a leader?

2. **FIGURE OUT WHO YOU'RE *NOT*.**
   Hey, it's great to be involved in the community. Bible studies are awesome. Students should memorize Scripture. Missions are essential. Drama. Worship. Theology. Evangelism. Leadership training. Family education. Book studies. You could possibly pick one of these, get online right now, and read an article on why it's vital for your student ministry (and why the church is failing because we don't do it enough). But that doesn't mean you should create a program for each one.

Bottom line: ⟶ **START DOING THINGS ON PURPOSE.**

It is so freeing to figure out your unique placement in the student ministry world. It keeps you from burning out, thinking you have to do everything (and be everything). It keeps you from feeling jealous and possessive of your program because you know it's not the answer for everybody.

FOUR: NEVER STOP LEARNING

In our experience, one of the main ways student pastors form their playbook is from *feedback*. Think about it. You—or someone you know—had an idea. Maybe it went something like this: "What if we did small groups after the sermon on Wednesday nights?" So you tried it one Wednesday. Later that night as the crowd was dwindling, you asked some of your lingering students, "How did you like going to small group after the talk?" And you, like any good leader, took their feedback into consideration. Maybe you sent a text the next day, getting reactions from an additional student or two. And all of that helped you decide if you were going to continue attempting small groups.

There are probably lots of things you do that were solidified through feedback. And that's okay. It's normal and healthy. Other than comparing week-to-week attendance or trying to emotionally gauge the room, how else are you going measure the effectiveness of your program?

In my (Kevin) environment, we're constantly asking the million-dollar question: "So, what did you think?" In other words, did that idea work? Was it helpful? Did it connect, or was it a total waste of everyone's time? And we employ that feedback to make vital decisions.

Would it be an exaggeration to say that a lot of student ministries are formed *completely* by feedback? And it almost always begins with a conversation.

- A student says, "There's not enough worship music." So you add songs and turn up the intensity.
- A volunteer leader thinks you should have more "fun" games in the program. So you put more planning and resources into game time.
- Your spouse believes that students need to be on stage and lead more. So you incorporate more student-led services.
- Your pastor tells you that you're not doing enough outreach events. So you add a "Serve the Community" night to your weekly schedule.

- A student's mom sends you an email explaining how she doesn't think your environment is "deep" enough. So you start teaching on more intellectual topics.

You get the idea. After a while (without even noticing it) your entire student environment is formed. Positive and negative feedback steer the ship.

BUT THERE'S A DIFFERENCE BETWEEN FEEDBACK AND *STRATEGIC* FEEDBACK.

And once you start doing things on purpose, as we talked about in the previous chapter, strategic feedback can take your environment to the next level.

Here are some ideas to get you started:

- Invite someone to come in and look at your environment with fresh eyes.
- Ask your most trusted volunteer: "What's the worst part of our program?"
- Ask another student pastor to observe your student ministry and then answer these two questions:

  1. What do I need to keep doing?
  2. What do I need to stop doing?

- Target influential freshman and sophomores who are new to your environment. They represent students who can sway a crowd, and—this is the cool part—they'll be around for a while to make an impact. And because they're new to your program, they won't be speaking from the perspective of a student who's simply "bored" with what you do and wants to try something different.

Ask questions like:

1. "Why are you here?" If you can find out why they showed up, it might give you a clue on how to reach more students like them?
2. "Did you have fun?" If they didn't have fun, they won't put their reputations on the line and invite their friends. This opens the door for you to ask questions about what they liked and disliked.

I (Kevin) ask about music, videos, games, and speakers. Because here's what I believe: **The better the execution of a strategy, the more effective the student ministry.** And the more student pastors hear words like *better* and *effective,* the longer they'll stay in the game.

I'm not saying that you need everybody's opinion. I'm saying that you need feedback that will enhance your strategy.

If you leave student ministry, Sister Kittie Loo will take the helm.

Instead, imagine three things you'd do if you believed you'll be here forever:

1.

2.

3.

YOU WILL
LEAVE
ONE DAY

The Problem With Doing It All

When I (Ben) was still in college, I spoke at a Wednesday night student gathering at a church in the Northwest. About an hour before the program started, the student pastor smiled at me and said, "Just so you know, it's a big deal that I'm letting you speak. I don't give up my pulpit much."

To which I responded, "How gracious of God to put the pulpit singularly under your pastoral possession."

I'm just kidding. I didn't respond at all. I couldn't think of anything to say. One, I had never heard a student pastor use the word *pulpit* to describe the communication portion of his or her program. Two, I felt my blood pressure rise. I was unseasoned as a communicator. I was truly afraid that I was going to somehow degrade *his* pulpit.

I honestly don't think that student pastor intended to sound arrogant or prideful (he was a solid guy). I think he was stating a literal fact: he did it *all*. Other people never spoke to his students. He communicated every week. He also connected with every student, communicated with every parent or stepparent, and planned every program.

He was a student pastor rock star.

I knew this guy—he didn't have a desperate need for the spotlight. That was simply the way he saw student ministry modeled. When he was in middle school and high school, his student pastor probably operated that way. The student pastor who came before him may have led that way, too. He probably considered "doing it all" to be his job, and he was merely working hard.

But within a year of my visit to his church, he burned out and changed professions completely.

I (Kevin) see this all the time—not just in churches but also in the way we student pastors are taught and educated. It's nobody's fault. It's just the way student ministry has always been done.

You're expected to:

- Talk and pray with every student who's ready to accept Christ.
- Handle (or fix) every student's problem at home or school.
- Speak every week.
- Go to every game, play, recital, etc.
- Have some type of athletic ability (at least enough to help the church softball team).
- Be able to dance, rap, or lead worship (maybe all three or maybe all three at the same time).
- Dress professionally, but still dress cool enough to appeal to students (which means *slim fit* but not *skinny* jeans).
- Keep up with culture, but don't endorse it (which means Justin Bieber was okay before he got the Jesus tattoo on his leg).

Add that to leading every mission trip, planning every retreat, and building every social media site, and it's no wonder so many of us are exhausted!

This isn't a book about having margin and resisting burning out, but those are certainly serious issues for people in our profession. And we want to help. **Since we've already decided that you want to do this job forever—or at least for a long time—maybe one of the best things you can do is start acting like you will leave one day.**

The Rock Star Mentality

Let's talk about obscure 90's bands, shall we? When I (Ben) was a freshman in high school, the band Blind Melon came out with the song "No Rain." I couldn't get enough of it. That's the song I currently sing to my one-year old when I rock her to sleep at night.

In 1995, I went to a Blind Melon concert in Atlanta, Georgia. They opened for a band called Silverchair. If you're a product of 90's alternative music, you're totally tracking with me. If not, just humor me. A couple weeks later, Blind Melon's lead singer Shannon Hoon died of an overdose. It was tragic.

The band is still a "functioning entity" to this day. You can go to their fan site, beemelon.com, where fans lovingly refer to themselves as Melonheads. But most of them would be quick to agree: it just hasn't been the same since Hoon's passing. They've tried and tried, but they haven't experienced the same success without him.

I listened—and still listen—to Blind Melon because of Shannon Hoon. I went to the concert in Atlanta because of Shannon Hoon. When he passed away, my interest in the band faded. The albums I own are the ones with him as the front man. I don't even know the name of the albums that came after. *That* is a rock star. He or she *is* the show.

 It totally makes sense in the music industry. But it doesn't make sense in student ministry.

Remember the student pastor I mentioned in the previous chapter? It was sad for me to see him fade out—exhausted. But there was another, even sadder reality—seeing the student ministry after he left. Because it was built 100 percent around his personality (and he had a good one), all the mojo left when he did. As the church scrambled to find a new personality to match his, the student ministry dwindled. It didn't pick up until they found another guy who could do it all—plus a little bit more.

So, what do you think happened to the students who were in the middle of this transition? How do you think his leaving impacted *them*?

If you make believe that you'll leave one day, you will build something that can outlast you. And the only way to build something that will outlast you is to find people who will outlast you.

For the record, "planning for the future" doesn't mean this:

Finding a replacement equal to you when you decide to move on.

This is a better way to plan for the future:

Finding leaders better than you right now, while you still work here.

We'll talk much more about this. But for right now, instead of thinking of yourself as a rock star, think of yourself like Fleetwood Mac, the Beach Boys, or even The Band (you know The Band, right? Remember the song "The Weight"? "Take a load off Annie!" Go ahead, sing it as loud as you possibly can!). Those groups were successful without having a front man. Who knows, maybe they were successful *because* of it. If those bands are too old, think about One Direction.

On second thought, don't think about One Direction.

Build A Bigger Base

We're confident that you want to make God the biggest deal of your student ministry. There's no question of spiritual motivation.

But there is a question of strategy.

 As student pastors, we're always asking how to grow a bigger ministry in order to have a bigger impact, but we rarely ask how to grow a ministry that will outgrow and outlast us.

The answer is simple: create a bigger foundation. Find other leaders who can effectively reach and connect with more students than you can.

When you build a house, the first thing you do is establish the base: footings, foundation walls, beam pockets, slab, etc. These sustain the weight of the house as you build upward. The same thing is true for a skyscraper. It takes a deep foundation below the earth to support the weight of the building above the surface.

Most student ministries are built more like a game of Jenga. Their foundations are assembled around one to three full-time staff people, and if *any* key people are taken out of the construction, the whole thing could come crumbling down.

If you want to build a bigger house or a taller building, you need a larger base and more support beams:

The more healthy leaders you have = the more students you can effectively reach
The more students you can effectively reach = the larger you can grow in a healthy way

Don't misunderstand—you *can* grow without great leaders. If you have one dynamic communicator or visionary with huge ideas and the resources to pull them off, you can build a big student ministry. But without multiple, healthy leaders, burnout is likely. Some students will fall through the cracks. And eventually, the ministry will face a decline.

Just a few years after its formation, North Point was well established as a large, influential congregation in the area. I (Kevin) was leading the student ministry when we launched our second campus, and then a third. Our family ministry environments were thriving, and the student ministry was growing fast.

After a few years, the student ministry director at our third campus, Clay Scroggins, and I decided to switch campuses. I won't bore you with the details that formed this decision, but it was essentially an equal trade. We were both ready to make a change.

Not everyone was entirely thrilled about the idea of this change. No one doubted Clay's ability as a leader, but I had been at the home campus since its beginning. The general feeling was that if you moved the original leader out of the foundation, some cracks would eventually form.

We did it anyway. And guess what? No one missed a beat.

Seriously.

Granted, everyone wants to be missed when they move out of a role. And I was no different. It was nice to receive encouragement through thank-you notes and emails. But more importantly, it was a great feeling when the ministry didn't suffer. The next week happened as usual, and the week after, and the week after that.

Both campuses thrived under new leadership and the students continued as if nothing had happened. For them, it was a non-event.

That transition was confirmation of something I learned several years prior: **don't build the ministry around you.** That lesson applies when it comes to dynamic worship leaders, engaging communicators, and visionary trailblazers. Clay and I were both responsible and involved leaders, but the student ministries we led weren't built around us or our personalities. Students saw *other* people lead worship, heard *other* people speak, and connected to *other* people in their small groups. That way, the foundation of our ministry stayed the same no matter how the pieces were rearranged.

Whether it's next week, five years from now, or when you're 85 years old, you will leave one day. With that in mind, here's a question to answer in the present:

Will the student ministry survive after you leave? Student ministries that are built on rock star personalities have a ceiling of 30 core students. If the rock star leaves, that student ministry will inevitably dwindle to 15 students. We've all seen it happen.

You may ask, "What if the church finds a dynamic replacement after I leave?" That's great, but here's the problem. The replacement—as great as he or she may be—isn't you. And if your tenure is built around you, it won't be built around him or her.

Stepping off the rock-star platform isn't always fun. It's nice to have students adore you. It's nice to be in control of every environment and be seen as a hard worker. But it's nicer to know that there's a strong, healthy, big team behind you. Think about the benefits.

- You won't be exhausted (and your family won't be frustrated).
- Your program will be able to grow in a healthy way.
- Your student ministry will still be standing when you walk away.

Many of you are already doing this well. You've found a number of ways to build healthy, vibrant student ministries around a solid foundation of leaders. We don't pretend to have all the answers when it comes to student ministry, but here are three ideas we've found to be helpful in building a bigger and stronger foundation.

IF YOU MAKE BELIEVE THAT YOU'LL LEAVE ONE DAY, YOU WILL . . .

ONE: RE-PRIORITIZE YOUR TIME

I (Ben) love seeing student pastors in action with their students. It's awe-inspiring. Lots of people in the outside world hear the word "teenager" and start frowning. One day I was talking to a guy next to me on an airplane. He asked what I do for a living. For some reason, I get nervous when people ask me that question. It's hard to explain to someone who's not in the church world. But I gave it my best shot. Here's how he responded: "I don't know how you do that. It's hard for me to even be around teenagers. I worry about the future of our nation."

If that guy knew some of the teenagers I know, he'd have a lot more hope. And that's exactly what I told him.

There's a reason you do what you do for a living. You probably enjoy being around teenagers. That's probably why you got into this profession in the first place. But spending time with students shouldn't be your only calling.

If you make yourself believe you're going to leave one day, you'll experience a mental shift that can help your ministry win right now. It may feel counterintuitive, but this single flip of priorities can set up your student ministry for years of success—with or without you.

→ SPEND MORE TIME WITH LEADERS THAN STUDENTS.

If you're just getting started in student ministry and you're wondering where to start, I suggest beginning with praying like crazy. Right after that, I suggest spending quality time with current and potential small group leaders.

If you're part of a team launching a church plant and you're wondering how to begin a student ministry from scratch, you should start by looking for solid small group leaders. Hang out with *them* (adult leaders) even before you start hanging out with students at Friday night football games.

Most new student pastors go straight for the students. Most church plants immediately form social gatherings of five to ten teenagers. That's fine, but **it would be better to start with a group of leaders than a group of students.** Then, as a team, you can take the student world by storm.

Think in terms of multiple leaders, not individual leadership. Again, we're not saying there shouldn't be a pastor or a point person. If you're currently recruiting leaders, you know it takes a strong leader to lead other leaders. You should be *most* intentional about investing in the people who invest in students.

If you're a student pastor, the job of recruiting key leaders ultimately rests on your shoulders. Don't be passive about hoping someone feels sorry for you and signs up to help. No, go after great people! Actively recruit them. Invest in them. Appreciate them. Lead them well so they will lead your students well.

If you want your ministry to thrive when you leave one day, this is your first move. And it's going to take some time.

So get started!

"Empowerment
is all about
letting go so
that others can
get going."

—KENNETH BLANCHARD

TWO: SHARE THE SPOTLIGHT

"Empowerment is all about letting go so that others can get going."
—Kenneth Blanchard

Maybe it's cheesy. But maybe, just maybe, you ought to frame that quote and put it on your wall.

If you believe that you're going to leave one day, you can't be satisfied with *only* empowering small group leaders. You must also look for talented communicators, worship leaders, musicians, videographers, sound techs, coffee brewers, and t-shirt designers.

I (Kevin) am constantly looking for talent. When I find someone, I give him or her a shot. Don't get me wrong. I never say, "Here's the microphone. Go for it." No, I'm *protective* of what happens on stage. But I'm not *possessive*.

One thing we can all do, starting today, is **look for talent.**

It's not just about on-stage talent. Look for visionaries, strategists, event planners and designers—leaders who have the ability to take things up a notch.

Finding and developing talent is risky and challenging. Talented communicators typically like to preach about what they like to preach about. That's not always best for the flow of a student ministry. Also, visionary leaders are characteristically very strong-willed and opinionated. We've probably all seen some near disasters when new people are given a shot. Let's be honest, some of us *were* disasters when someone first gave us a shot.

But in spite of the challenges, developing leaders is worth it.
- Summer camps are full of speakers and worship leaders who were discovered by *someone*.
- Churches are benefitting from staff members who were developed by *someone*.

→ **TALENTED PEOPLE AREN'T IN THESE POSITIONS BECAUSE THEY STUMBLED UPON A GREAT GIG. IT'S BECAUSE SOMEONE FOUND THEM, TOOK A RISK ON THEM, AND HAD THE GRACE AND PATIENCE TO STICK WITH THEM.**

Whether your setting is rural or urban, whether your student ministry is big or small, whether your budget is thriving or nonexistent, there is always talent available. You just have to find it.

In my (Ben) first student ministry job, our budget was $25 a week. We bought Mountain Lightning and Dr. Thunder instead of Mountain Dew and Dr. Pepper. Thank you, Walmart. We had zero full-time people—student ministry was one of my ten job responsibilities. It wasn't easy, but we *never* **let one communicator speak more than 50 percent of the time.**

I still abide by that same rule today.

When you step out of your current role, you don't want to take all of the talent and leadership with you. So find someone with potential. Give someone a chance. Help someone grow in front of your eyes.

Bottom line: **start recruiting.** Here are four simple ways:

1. Let someone speak who's not as gifted as you and help them get better.
2. Let someone other than you make decisions, challenge processes, and give feedback.
3. Let your best leaders start mentoring new people.
4. Diversify your platform. Talent comes in all genders, ages, colors, styles, and backgrounds. And chances are your students do, too.

[THREE:] CHECK YOUR EGO

Track with me (Ben) for a second. Let's say you acted on what you read in the previous chapter. Just pretend like you thought it was a good idea. You gave multiple people an opportunity to communicate in your environment. And let's say two or three of those communicators did a solid job. That's great, right? If you're the primary speaker, that means you now have two or three *other* voices who can help you carry that load. All of a sudden, you have more time to invest in students, connect with parents, and recruit great leaders.

But what if one of those communicators turned out to be *really great?* Like, they thoroughly knocked it out of the park. Students were engaged. Small groups were winning. People were doing fist pumps on the days they found out this particular speaker was delivering the message.

I have a big question for you. And I want you to be super honest with yourself about the answer:

$\longrightarrow$ **WOULD YOU BE EXCITED OR DISAPPOINTED?**

Would it be difficult for you to celebrate their success? Would it be challenging for you to let them outshine you?

If you answered, "No, it wouldn't even be a little bit challenging," you're either on your way to sainthood or you're not self-aware. I (Ben) have had to look inside myself and answer that question a lot. I've almost always worked in environments with multiple communicators. I've seen students tweet other speakers and say things like, "Awesome message 2nite. Ur my favorite speaker."

I remember the first time I spoke at North Point Community Church. I overheard a sophomore guy in the hallway look at his small group leader and yell, "Stuart Hall's *not* speaking tonight. Gah! This is so stupid!" And he stormed out. True story.

Not an easy task—following Stuart Hall. It's like when Alex Linz replaced Macaulay Culkin in *Home Alone 3*. Ever heard of *Home Alone 3?* Exactly.

Listen, sometimes in ministry we need to learn to loosen our grip— to not hold on too tightly. We need to own our jealousy, battle our insecurity, and check our ego at the door.

Being competitive is great. Wanting to be the best is perfectly normal. **But sometimes the best thing you can do as a student pastor is channel your competitiveness towards something bigger than yourself.** Think of it this way: if another communicator succeeds in your environment, you succeed. If they effectively teach students, then you have done a marvelous job of teaching students in your program. Everybody wins.

When I hear communicators speak who are better than me (which happens more than I'd like to admit), I try to learn something from them that can help me. When I overheard that student complaining in the hallway at North Point, I made a mental note to pay close attention when Stuart spoke. He was doing something right.

But when I hear communicators preach that are better than me *in an environment that I'm responsible for,* I don't just celebrate. I do a backflip! Ok, not really. But I get excited.

It takes serious heart-work to truly embrace Proverbs 29:25, *"Fear of man will prove to be a snare, but whoever trusts in the Lord is kept safe."* It requires some changes in your thought-life and prayer-life. But if you can do it, look at the payoff—you're *safe.* Safe from anxiety. Safe from insecurity. Safe from the pressure of being "the one." And more importantly, your student ministry is safe, too.

Clothe yourself in humility.

Find joy in seeing other people succeed.

Brag on them.

Celebrate them.

And maybe they'll help your student ministry thrive—while you're there *and* long after you leave.

If you don't recruit great leaders, you'll build the student ministry around you.

If you build the student ministry around you, your students will quit coming to church when you leave.

If your students quit coming to church when you leave, they'll start making foolish decisions.

If they start making foolish decisions, they'll end up in prison.

If they end up in prison, they'll join inmate gangs and get tattoos of angry clowns.

Don't let your students join inmate gangs and get tattoos of angry clowns.

Recruit great leaders.

Write the name of the person who took a chance on you.

Write the name of someone you're currently investing in.

Write the name of someone you need to take a chance on.

YOUR SENIOR PASTOR IS RIGHT

Who's Responsible?

Submitting to authority is easy.

. . . as long as you like your authority.
. . . and they're asking you to do something you want to do.
. . . and you gain something in the process.
. . . and you feel heard, respected and valued the entire time.

On second thought, maybe submitting to authority isn't so easy.
Because let's be honest—there's something in all of us that wants to
do, well . . . whatever we want.
We don't like being told what to do.
We don't like being told when to do it.
We don't like being told who to do it with.
We don't like having to say yes.
We don't like hearing the word no.

The apostle Paul penned a letter to his friends in the Thessalonian
church. Even though they were a intelligent group of Christians,
some areas of their lives (and church) were in complete chaos. Paul
tackled a wide assortment of issues, ranging from sexual purity to the
Rapture. He also addressed their attitude towards church leaders:

> *Now we ask you, brothers and sisters, to acknowledge those who
> work hard among you, who care for you in the Lord and who
> admonish you. Hold them in the highest regard in love because of
> their work. Live in peace with each other. (I Thessalonians 5:12-13)*

In summary, I think Paul was asking his friends to do three things:
1. Appreciate your leaders for their work.
2. Choose to love your leaders because of their work.
3. Have a good attitude toward your leaders because of their work.

Notice a theme here—*because of their work*. You don't always love and respect your leaders because they're easy to love and easy to respect. You do it because they serve people. They help families and marriages heal. They show communities the love of Christ. They offer hope to individuals in hopeless situations. *That's* why you honor and submit to them.

You don't know how much the morale of your church could improve if you honored and submitted to your senior pastor.

You don't know the types of problems that could emerge from your negativity towards your senior pastor.

You don't know how effective your church could be if the two of you were unified.

You don't know hard it will be for your church to do its best work if the two of you are divided.

It's easy to talk about your senior pastor or executive pastor and all the things they do wrong or insufficiently. But this book isn't written to them. It's for you. The goal is for you to take a look at yourself and discern the areas where you could improve.

 Put the responsibility of respecting authority on your own shoulders. Make yourself believe in God-ordained biblical authority. You could focus all your attention on your leaders—their strengths and weaknesses. Instead, focus it on your faith, your actions

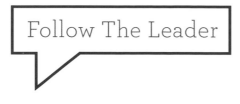

Follow The Leader

I (Ben) love hanging out with student pastors. In fact, I've never had a desire to do anything other than student ministry. Sure, making more money would be nice. But other than that, I can't think of a better job.

But I've noticed recently that a lot of my conversations with student pastors have gone like this:
Them: *If you know of any job openings, let me know.*
Me: *Everything okay?*
Them: *Oh yeah. Our student ministry is awesome! Better than it's ever been. I'm just not sure about the rest of the church.*

Most of the time, that conversation ends with two simple ideas from the student pastor:

1. **The senior pastor needs to go.**
2. **I need to be in charge.**

Maybe you feel this way right now. I've been there. I remember a time early in my career when I thought I should run the church.

I'm so glad I didn't. There are lots of reasons why, but I'll pick one.

Let's say I became the key leader as soon as I thought I deserved it. How insecure would I be the second I hired my first staff members? I'd wonder they were thinking the exact same things that I thought: *I would do a better job of being senior pastor than Ben. My department is great—it's the rest of the church that I'm worried about.*

If you hijack your senior pastor's leadership right now, you might become paranoid when you become a senior pastor later. Sure, you'll be in charge. You'll have the power to change the way things are done, and you'll have people who follow you. But there will be a nagging insecurity that comes with it. Because you'll know the way that you thought about (and yes, talked about) your leader. Maybe you'll wonder if your student pastor is thinking those things about you.

If you don't want to follow *now*, does that make you qualified to lead *later?*
Probably not.

One day Jesus was invited to eat at the house of a well-known Pharisee. But this wasn't a one-on-one lunch. It was more like a dinner party. Jesus watched as guests clamored to seat themselves as close as possible to the host. In that culture, the closer you were to the host, the higher your status. So Jesus seized the opportunity to teach on humility:

When someone invites you to a wedding feast, do not take the place of honor, for a person more distinguished than you may have been invited. If so, the host who invited both of you will come and say to you, 'Give this person your seat.' Then, humiliated, you will have to take the least important place. But when you are invited, take the lowest place, so that when your host comes, he will say to you, 'Friend, move up to a better place.' Then you will be honored in the presence of all the other guests. For all those who exalt themselves will be humbled, and those who humble themselves will be exalted (Luke 14:7-11).

What a great passage to remind us all to check our motives!

To paraphrase . . .

you can make yourself a big deal	OR	**you can be a big deal where you are and wait for someone to promote you**

Maybe, just maybe, **the quicker you learn to follow, the sooner you will be ready to lead**. Start by focusing on these three things:

- **Self-awareness.** Build your emotional intelligence. Pay attention to yourself and the way you come across as a follower. What are your weaknesses as an employee? How can you get better at being led?
- **Humility.** We've hit this nail several times already. Work out your humility muscle as hard as you possibly can. Pray for more humility, and then train yourself to get stronger in this area.
- **Patience.** The Bible has a lot to say about patience. Here's a quick sample: *Better a patient person than a warrior (Proverbs 16:32)*. Most of us want to be warriors. And though being patient isn't quite as glamorous, according to the Bible, it's better.

You know where we came up with these three ideas? From you. Many of you have taught us how to navigate the complex senior pastor/ student pastor relationship. You're already doing this in such an incredible way that we were inspired to challenge *everyone* to follow your lead.

Walk In His Shoes

Do you ever criticize the president of the United States? Don't answer that. Just think about it. Have you ever gotten wrapped up in a conversation about politics—policy, morality, military, the economy, and other words that end in *y*—and found yourself critical of his leadership? Did you do that with the president before him and the president before him?

Here's a gross understatement: none of us know what it's like to wear his shoes. Behind closed doors—which are probably behind three sets of steel, bullet proof doors—it's impossible to know what it's *really* like. But standing a million degrees of separation away from him, trying to sound smart at the water cooler, it's easy to cast stones.

We're not making any political statements by the way. We're just making the point that talking *about* somebody is much different than *being* somebody.

That truth also applies to your senior pastor. We realize the illustration doesn't line up perfectly because you have direct access to him. But still, you're not wearing his shoes. As close as the two of you may be, you're not him.

Ron Edmondson, pastor of Immanuel Baptist Church in Lexington, Kentucky, wrote a blog on churchleaders.com titled "10 Secrets Many Senior Pastors Keep." His list was eye-opening and thought-provoking. Read it through the filter of walking in your senior pastor's shoes:

1. Leading from this position is overwhelming at times. We know Christ is ultimately in charge, but we also know it often seems everyone looks to us to have all the answers.

2. People tell the senior pastor all kinds of things about what is happening in their life or in the lives of others . . . many we would rather not know sometimes . . . and sometimes the weight of others problems we carry is enormous.

3. Most pastors walk with a degree of uncertainty, which keeps us in prayer, but also makes us question our abilities at times. It makes depression common for many senior pastors.

4. Many senior pastors fear the possibility of failing in their role, so they thrive on the encouragement and prayers of others.

5. Sometimes we allow insecurity to cause us to become overprotective of our reputation and our position.

6. We face the same temptations and occasional spiritual dryness as everyone else. This means we need accountability, but are often afraid to seek it.

7. Our spouse is sometimes the loneliest person in the church and often feels extreme pressure to live up to unrealistic expectations.

8. Loneliness can exist for all leaders and many pastors suffer from it.

9. We seldom know who we can trust, which is why we become guarded and appear hard to get to know. Most senior pastors have been burned by someone they once trusted.

10. We suspect the staff, church leaders and congregation sometimes talks about us behind our back.

Wow. What a list. When we emailed Ron and asked him for permission to use excerpts of his blog in this book—and threw a couple other questions at him—he sent back this reply: *"I think many student pastors have aspirations to be a senior pastor. Learning the unique tensions early could help them in the future. Plus, many student pastors see only the concerns of their own ministry, and wonder why they aren't more supported. They don't see the weight or width of decisions their senior pastor deals with."*

Bottom line: **THERE ARE TWO SIDES TO THIS COIN . . . YOU NEED TO LOOK AT BOTH OF THEM.**

Your senior pastor is flawed. He probably has some blind spots and deficient areas of leadership. But don't forget: *he's a human being.* Check your expectations of him. As you can see by this list, he has a lot going on.

Currently you are dealing with things in your ministry area that, no matter how hard your senior pastor tries, he doesn't fully understand. The reverse is true as well. You simply cannot completely comprehend some of the pressures, fears, relational challenges, and insecurities that he faces.

Live What You Want Them To Learn

I (Ben) have been speaking to students since 1998. I don't want to over-exagerrate, but my guess is that I've preached more than 50 sermons on the subject of authority. Submission. Respect. Making the first move. Humility. Apologizing. Fighting for the relationship instead of fighting to be right. Etc. Etc. Etc.

Students are under all types of authority: traditional parents, stepparents, mom's third husband, dad's live-in girlfriend, grandparents, teachers, coaches, tutors, band directors, on and on we could go. Some of that authority is great. Some of it is challenging at best. But even when students' authority is depraved, it doesn't change the message, does it? We don't tell students, "Never mind, you're exempt from honoring *them*." **The Bible doesn't suddenly become irrelevant because a teenager faces an insolent authority figure**. In fact, the more complex the authority, the more impactful the truth can be.

When Paul said, *"Let every person be subject to the governing authorities. For there is no authority except from God, and those that exist have been instituted by God" (Romans 13:1)*, he wasn't writing to a church that was under a fair, peaceful, humble and kind government. Let's just call it what it was—they were under Emperor Nero.

As challenging as your senior pastor is, you most likely haven't nicknamed him Nero! (Wait . . . you haven't, have you?)

Here's the point: if you stand in front of teenagers and tell them to respect and submit to their parents and stepparents, don't you think it would be of utmost importance for you to put those same principles in action? You have to live what you want them to learn Don't look students in the eye and tell them to fight for their relationship with their parents, and then turn around and throw that truth out the window because you don't like the way your senior pastor overmanages or undermanages you.

I'll say it again: live what you want them to learn.

If you're sitting there thinking, *I've never actually preached a sermon on respecting authority,* congratulations—your next series is now planned! As you prepare for it, let the truths you encounter sink in and lead your heart in a better direction.

With that being said, let's look at four specific behaviors that could help you live under the authority of your professional leader.

WHEN YOU MAKE BELIEVE YOUR SENIOR PASTOR IS RIGHT YOU WILL . . .

ONE: ASK THE QUESTION

If you're a leader or manager right now, wouldn't it be amazing if the people who reported to you looked for ways to serve you better? If they really listened to you and looked for ways to help you? Wouldn't that be encouraging?

Submission is easy to talk about. It's difficult, however, to put into practice.

Our senior pastor, Andy Stanley, has encouraged people in a variety of contexts—business, marriage, parenting, and ministry leadership—to ask this question:

→ WHAT CAN I DO TO HELP?

You should ask your senior pastor that question.

Like most acts of humility, this question is more impactful for the asker than it is for the answerer. If you choose to ask it, you'll immediately tune in to your senior pastor's needs instead of only focusing on your own. You'll be obliged to listen to his answer. You'll be forced to care. **Any time you're listening, tuning in and caring, you're practicing humility.**

The other day, a senior pastor complained to me (Ben) about his student pastor. Which is odd, because I usually hear the venting from the other side. I felt like I was betraying my tribe. The senior pastor grumbled about the fact that his student pastor never helps him. I don't remember the conversation verbatim, but here's a paraphrase:

> *When I started in student ministry 40 years ago, it was an unsaid expectation that I would carry the pastor's briefcase for him. He was my authority, and that was one of the ways I showed him respect. My student pastor doesn't even help me move tables or stack chairs. He just stands there and talks to me. I don't get it. He loves to talk, but he never asks if there's anything he can do for me.*

I realize that carrying someone's briefcase is an old school idea. I don't even know where someone would *buy* a briefcase. But if standing around while a senior pastor stacks chairs is new school, I'd rather be antiquated.

You may be thinking, *I would never do that.* But what if you already are? In your own way, **what if you're standing by and watching in an area where you could be extremely helpful?**

You'll never know until you ask.

TWO: THE 40-LIST

Throughout the course of a year (or two if necessary), work hard to learn some new things *from* your senior pastor—either through conversation, information or observation. The goal is to glean 40 new insights.

As you go, list them in a Word doc in your computer.

But here's the kicker—don't make them negative. For instance:

Don't write: *I learned that it would be terrible for me to micromanage my student pastor if I ever became a senior pastor.*

Maybe that is something you learned. But it's not for this list. Here's a better example:

Do write: *Go to your kids' important events, even if you have to cancel meetings.*

Even if you're not married and you don't have kids right now, that's still an awesome thing for you to learn from your senior pastor.

What you learn could be . . .
- **personal:** marriage, parenting, money, etc.
- **spiritual:** prayer, Bible reading, character, etc.
- **professional:** business, leadership, pastoring, etc.

No matter who you're senior pastor is, you can pick up 40 positive things from him. And when you do, print out two copies of your list. Laminate one and put it in your desk. Frame the other one and put it on a wall in a place where you can see it regularly. It will remind you of two things:
1. Learning from someone is better than criticizing them.
2. Your senior pastor is smart.

And in many ways, he's right.

THREE: LEARN SOMETHING TOGETHER

Learning is a big deal. It takes humility. When you stop learning, you're essentially saying, "I'm good—got it all figured out."

We've talked about learning *from* your senior pastor. Now imagine if you could learn *with* your senior pastor:

- Which books have been impactful for him? Ask him if he'd be willing to take you through one. You don't have to put massive pressure on yourselves to go ten layers deep into every chapter. It just needs to be something you do together. It could be a book on personal faith, ministry systems, leadership, business, money, or the dawn of jazz music in post World War I Britain.
- Listen to a podcast or sermon separately, then get together and talk about it.
- Take a class or go through leadership training together.

We've been through several books with various pastors at our church. Most of the books were more helpful than they were mind-blowing. But hearing our pastors process them through the lens of our church was enlightening. It gave us something common to talk about. It focused our planning around ideas from the book instead of revolving it around competing opinions.

If you hate and disagree with everything we say in this book, and your one takeaway is to keep learning, we're okay with that. Actually we're not, but we do want you to make it a habit. As we said in section one, **leaders use their imagination to spark faith in others. And one of the best ways you can strengthen your imagination is by learning.**

We want you to take some steps towards learning with your senior pastor. If that's impossible, we still want you to build that muscle in your own life.

FOUR: FOLLOW

Follow like you want to be followed one day.

That's it.

If you don't like working with other people, here's a new job for you to consider:

Tire North Ltd., a division of Kingland Ford Group of Companies in Hay River, Northwest Territories (Canada), is looking for a **Tire Technician's Trainee** at their remote mine site.

Here's the link for you to apply: http://ca.indeed.com/cmp/Kingland-Ford-Sales-Ltd./jobs/Tire-Technician-Trainee-0ecbf200fb45b449

Or

You could imagine ways to improve your professional relationship now. *What are three ways you can serve your senior pastor?*

1.

2.

3.

YOUR CHILDREN'S PASTOR IS COOL

Children's Pastors Have A Tough Job

When you think about it, being a children's pastor is tough.

1. **They rarely get weeks off.** Some of you have the option to cancel your student environment for major holidays. Not so in children's ministry. As long as there are Sunday church services, there will be a fully functioning children's program.

2. **Parents of kids are different than any other species on Earth.** They still have parent goggles on—everything their child does is world altering. I (Kevin) can make fun of them because I've been there. I (Ben) can make fun of me because I'm living it right now. When kids get to middle school and high school, most parents begin to set the bar at a more realistic level. But when they're young, parents are convinced that their kid. Is. The. Greatest.

   For example, parents who have a child who loves to draw or paint will describe their kid as an "incredible artist." That's great—it's healthy to affirm and encourage kids. But just because kids draw distinguishable cats and trees doesn't mean they're the next James McNeill Whistler or Andy Warhol. You just can't convince parents of that. That's why being a little league baseball coach is a lot of pressure—because *all* parents see their kid as a future hall of famer. And if you don't see it, you're the devil. Parents are much more involved, and much more, how shall we say it, *eager*.

3. **There are unique stresses that come with being a children's pastor.** First, the communication obstacles. Most teenagers will tell you if they have an intense food allergy. Most young kids, on

the other hand, will eat any cupcake you put in their hands—even if eating it will put them in the emergency room.

Second, kids' developmental stages. As a student pastor, you have to learn teenage culture. Similarly, a children's pastor has to learn psychological and intellectual development. If you think it's difficult to take complex theological ideas and make them digestible for a sophomore, imagine doing it for a five-year old. If you think it's challenging to address divorce and tragedy with teenagers, try tackling those topics with first graders.

Third, safety. Think about the pressure of high-attendance services. For you, the main challenges are overcrowded small groups and insufficient Mountain Dew cans. For children's pastors, their challenges include missing kids and flailing meltdowns. Two words for you—*fire evacuation*. If you ever think your job is tough, picture that exercise with scores of confused preschoolers.

And if all of that doesn't sell you, think about this: Teenagers are potty trained.

The Importance Of Childhood

Think about one of the first questions you ask when a tragedy strikes: "What about the kids?" Nothing pulls on human heartstrings like children in unsafe situations. Similarly, nothing infuriates people more than their mistreatment. You can get together representatives from 20 different religions, and none of them will debate that children shouldn't be hurt.

Children are vulnerable. They're still forming their views on, well, everything. Between six months and eight years, the human brain goes from half its weight to 90 percent of its final weight. I guess that explains why eight-year olds seem to have heads that are way too big for their bodies. They all look a little bit like Dora the Explorer.

During this window of time while the brain takes shape, it's critical for a child's mind to wrap around the right stuff. Otherwise his or her brain has to rewire itself later, and that's a much bigger job.

R. S. Lee's book, *Your Growing Child and Religion,* confirms:

> *"The first seven years [of life] constitute the period for laying the foundations of religion. This is the most important period in the whole of a person's life in determining his later religious attitudes."* [1]

I (Kevin) know a lot of people who are going to church for the first time—or for the first time in decades—because they have kids. A dad told me the other day, "I want my kids to avoid the mistakes I've made." Even people who *don't* go to church think church is important for kids.

While the foundation of a child's future is being built, it's vital for him or her to have the right building blocks—socially, emotionally, intellectually, and yes, spiritually.

Bottom line: **YOUR CHILDREN'S PASTOR IS AN IMPORTANT PERSON.**

- What he or she teaches children about God—vital.
- What he or she teaches children about family, community, church, love, trust, faith, the Bible, and numerous virtues—critical.
- What he or she models and demonstrates to impressionable children—essential.

Serve Or Be Served

"Student pastors already think they know everything, so why even try?"

That's what someone told me (Ben) the other day. It's an unfair generalization, but it reveals the way a lot of people in the ministry world think about us. I don't agree with them, but I will admit this: I hesitate to ever get too many student pastors in the same room talking about the same thing—a fight breaks out every time!

I love that we are a group of people who are strong-willed and passionate. But no one wins if outsiders view people in our profession as prideful or arrogant. For many of us, it's time to grab some humility and hang on tight.

Think about what Jesus said when His disciples asked Him, *"Who, then, is the greatest in the kingdom of heaven?"* Jesus grabbed a volunteer out of the audience—a little kid, in fact—and quickly replied, *"Whoever takes the lowly position of this child is the greatest in the kingdom of heaven"* (Matthew 18:1-4). Enough said.

Not long after that, Jesus told some of His closest friends, *"And whoever wants to be first must be your slave—just as the Son of Man did not come to be served, but to serve, and to give his life as a ransom for many" (Matthew 20:27-28).* As *the* Champion of our faith, Jesus had every right to expect people to serve Him. Instead, He flipped that idea on its head.

Humility means serving other people, not just supporting yourself and your own ideas. **It means giving yourself up instead of building yourself up.** And it means respecting other people, wanting what's best for them, and helping them win.

Even if . . .

you don't feel respected by them.
they don't want what's best for you.
they take no steps to help you win.

But it's not easy. First, we're all hardwired to protect our own interests. Second, there's no guaranteed reciprocation. With no promise of payoff, it's hard to get motivated to do anything for someone else.

But here's the cool part: when you do this, it sets God up to be more heroic than you. And it models the character of Jesus to the people you work *for*, the people you work *with*, and the students who are watching you.

Benefits Of Working Together

Right now, your relationship with your children's pastor operates a certain way. For some of you, it's great. For others, it's nonexistent. Make believe that it's thriving and winning. Imagine how that would improve ...

1. **Transitions.** When it comes to helping kids move from children's ministry to student ministry, every church is different. Churches do it at different ages, and at different times of the year, but almost all of them do it. And it's a huge deal.

    This is so much easier when you have a good relationship with your children's pastor. First, he or she will be more open to letting you (or your students) get in front of their kids and promote your ministry. Second, things will happen so much faster and smoother. Why? Because you'll be able to coordinate details like ...

    dates
    communication to parents
    marketing

    And all of that will happen with much less tension and suspicion.

2. **Resources.** There will inevitably come a day when you want to use a room in the children's ministry area. For small group meeting space. A parent meeting. Mission trip planning. Child care for your volunteers. An arena for mixed martial arts. When you need to borrow a room, it will be a much easier request if you have relational change in your pocket with your children's pastor.

    Also, what about budget discussions? Aren't those the highlight of your mortal existence? Instead of living in constant tension with your children's pastor, what if you joined forces? Wouldn't that make budget discussions so much more amiable? And, at some point, wouldn't it help you catch a break?

3. **Volunteers.** You want great volunteers, teachers, and small group leaders. Guess what? So does your children's pastor. And you probably recognize when a potential leader doesn't "fit" in student ministry. Here's a hint: if they ask where you keep your felt board and finger painting supplies, you may want to introduce them to your children's pastor. Wouldn't it be awesome if you all were constantly on the lookout *for each other?*

4. **Service opportunities.** At the church I (Kevin) attend, our K–5th ministry, Upstreet, is full of high school students who serve on Sunday mornings. At one point, teenagers made up over 50% of Upstreet's volunteer base.

   It's a win-win. I look at our children's ministry director, Chad Ward, as a hero. Why? Because he provides a place for heaps of high school students to serve each week. He trains them, equips them, and gives them a role. As a result, those students develop a deeper faith.

   Even better, he sees me as a hero, too. Why? Because I'm so good-looking and cool. Just kidding. Because I endorse and encourage students to anchor his volunteer base. And he knows that children look at teenagers with stars in their eyes, and that students can bring energy and fun into a children's ministry like no one else can.

5. **Peace of mind.** In the end, getting along with your children's pastor is better for your mental health. It's better for the quality of your work environment. It's better for your church. And it's better for the parents who have children in both of your programs.

Here are four practical ways you can build a better relationship with your children's pastor. They're not the *only* four, but they'll get you started.

WHEN YOU MAKE BELIEVE YOUR CHILDREN'S PASTOR IS COOL, YOU . . .

ONE: CONNECT AS HUMAN BEINGS

It may seem like we're painting an unrealistic expectation for you and your children's pastor. You may be sitting there imagining *us* imagining the two of *you* hanging out every weekend, going on combined family vacations, and attending premieres of the newest *Marvel* movies.

But that's not our expectation. We know you're different. We know you're busy. Between all of your programs and responsibilities, there probably isn't time to develop a life-long friendship.

We're not asking you to make your children's pastor your #1 friend. We are, however, asking you to connect with him or her as a human being. Just take an interest in *one thing* they're interested in. It doesn't have to be church or ministry related. It could be anything:

- Politics
- Sports
- Pinterest
- Musical theater
- Chili Cook-Offs
- Disney movies
- Scrapbook conventions

The beauty is that you can get on your phone or computer and read a short blog post about something they like. You can do very little work and make a very big connection. Even a Google search will give you some substantial conversation topics.

This is why this is such a big deal: **because people love it when you take an interest in them.** When people feel noticed, listened to, and remembered, it has a bigger effect than you think. Why? Because it lets them know that they're valuable and important . . . not many things are more paramount than that. It doesn't matter people's age, gender, or profession, they like it when someone cares about them. You have the ability to do that with your children's pastor.

Or, maybe you could go to a scrapbook convention with him or her. *That* has the potential to change both of your lives forever!

TWO: WORK ON SOMETHING TOGETHER

Julian Reyes wrote an article in Salt Lake City's *Deseret News* that highlighted a recent project that brought together Iraqi and Utah students.[2] The program Bridge Over Barriers invited Iraqi high school students and their host families to paint a mural on a thoroughfare in hopes of closing the gap between cultures.

Notice that the avenue to connecting them *wasn't* a lecture. No one sat them down and forced them to wholly understand, agree with, or even like each other. The avenue was work. A job. A project.

I (Ben) have never seen students unify the way they do when they go on local or international mission trips. By working together, students with little in common and no previous relational history, come together. I find myself continually shocked by how richly mission trips boost relationships.

I think you could take a page out of that book. Here's what I'd love for you to do: **find something to work on together with your children's pastor.**

Maybe it's transitions or resources, like we previously mentioned. Maybe it's a church-wide service project. Maybe it's the improvement of a certain area on your church's property. Maybe it's uniting to recruit better players for your church softball team. It doesn't matter. All that matters is that the two of you get side-by-side and tackle a project together—same goal, shared responsibility.

Put your humility pants on and pray for the Spirit of God to be stronger than your pride. Then go, get on the same team, and work on something with your children's pastor.

THREE: **MAKE KIDS HEROES IN YOUR STUDENT MINISTRY**

The topic of kids can be handled in a lot of ways in your student
ministry. Kids can be . . .
ignored and never talked about.
mocked—the butt of jokes.
reluctantly tolerated.
a source of guilt.
Or they can be heroes.

Act like it's awesome to hang out with kids. A few ways you can do that:

- Don't talk negatively about kids during your sermons. Annoying
  younger siblings and stepsiblings are an easy target. Don't play
  that card.
- Show funny and cute, not annoying, YouTube videos of kids.
  There are a lot of hilarious videos highlighting kids doing
  ridiculous things. Show those instead of videos of kids screaming
  and pitching fits for a quick laugh.
- Interview influential students who volunteer with kids. Find guys
  and girls in your ministry who are decent at talking on stage and
  do a super-quick interview with them about how awesome it is to
  volunteer in children's ministry.
- On the flip side, bring in some kids to talk about how great
  it is to have teenagers who hang out with them. Remember
  the old show *Kids Say The Darndest Things?* It's true—they
  do. Find some kids who have big personalities, practice with
  them ahead of time, and then interview them during your main
  student environment.
- Publically talk about your children's pastor and children's
  ministry with respect. Public loyalty gives you private influence.

When you read the Gospels, you'll notice how Jesus elevated the
treatment of outcasts, widows, women, and sinners. But you'll also notice
that He raised the view of children by the way He accepted them.

Go and do the same thing.

FOUR: SERVE YOUR CHILDREN'S PASTOR

Did you ever watch *Extreme Makeover: Home Edition* on ABC? Ty Pennington runs around like a crazy man while local construction crews do ridiculous interior and exterior improvements on homes for less fortunate families and schools.

There's always a person or family who is the "Star" of each episode. And usually they have an exceptionally heartbreaking or inspiring story. The producer sends them on vacation while their home gets completely remodeled and rebuilt.

My (Ben) favorite part is when the family returns and the whole town comes out to watch as the new house in unveiled. I cry. Every. Single. Time.

What if you did that every once in a while—made your children's pastor the "Star" of the show? You don't have the time or resources to remodel their house, but you can do *something* that helps them. Start by asking yourself this question:

→ WHAT IS ONE THING I COULD DO ONE TIME THAT WOULD PROVIDE ONE HUGE BOOST FOR MY CHILDREN'S PASTOR?

Let's break that down . . .

One thing
One time
One huge boost

It needs to be something within your power. It needs to be something that you can pull off successfully. And it needs to be something that will make the children's pastor feel, as we call it in the church world, "blessed."

You're smarter than us, but here are five ideas to get your brain in motion:

1. Gather your students and improve or repair some part of the children's area at your church.
2. Have five or six of your students write the children's pastor a note to thank him or her for working with kids, especially their siblings.
3. Help your children's pastor coordinate a big push to get more volunteers.
4. Let your student ministry sponsor your church's summer VBS. Rally your students to help it win. Make it part of your student ministry summer calendar.
5. Put on a fundraiser to buy something special for the children's department.

Six Things You And Your Children's Pastor Could Learn Together At A Scrapbooking Convention:

1. When people say "punch", they're not commenting on the refreshments. It's a tool that instantly cuts out any shape you could possibly imagine.
2. Archival quality albums are *way* better than photo safe albums. Obviously.
3. Digital scrapbooking is a real thing. And no, it's not Instagram.
4. A *Cricut Machine* is the scrapbook equivalent of a 1970 Chevelle SS 454.
5. Scrapbooking, or "scrapping" as the professionals call it, is big business. A common fee to have your scrapbook created is $30 per page. There's a way to bolster your budget!
6. The most influential scrapbookers go on tour to meet their "fans". Yes, you read that correctly.

When you get back from the convention, take some time and brainstorm the answer to this question:

What is one thing you could do one time that would provide one huge boost for your children's pastor?

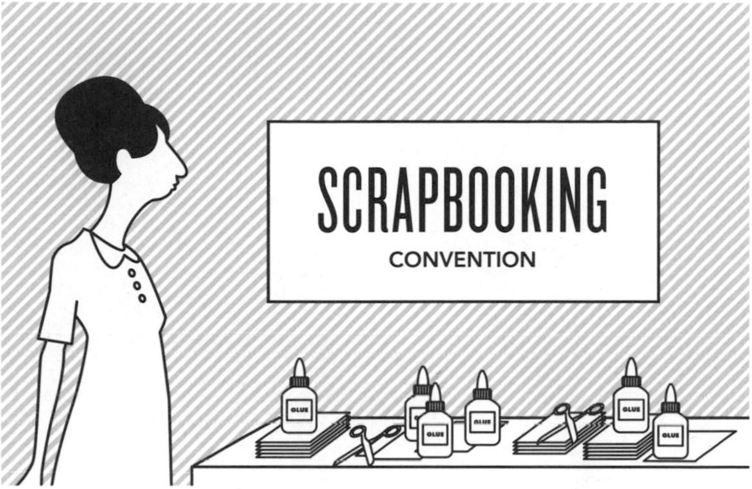
SCRAPBOOKING
CONVENTION

YOU NEED
PARENTS

Exceptions To The Rule

When it comes to parents, student pastors believe a lot of things. Some of them we're not sure we can print in this book.

But if we were to recap some of the statements we've heard when we talk to people who work with middle school and high school students, it would sound something like this:

- "Partnering with parents makes sense for preschool directors and children's pastors. But in student ministry, it's just not practical."

- "Parents of little kids are connected to our church—they drop off their children, care about the ministry, and actually know something about the Bible. In student ministry, they're completely disconnected."

- "A lot of students show up at our environment because a friend invited them. Or they're desperate for a date. Or they want a bus ticket to the beach for summer camp. Their parents don't even know where they are half the time."

- "The parents we deal with, aren't believers, are disengaged, are clueless, have a ridiculous amount of mess and baggage, and don't know how to relate to teenagers like we do."

There's some truth behind those beliefs. Interacting with parents of teenagers is much different than interacting with parents of preschoolers. Why? Because parenting is so different at that stage. So if you're in a church that values the idea of "family ministry," there's bound to be some frustration as you seek to partner with parents.

But even if those beliefs have *some* truth behind them, they don't tell the full story. All too often we focus on the exception instead of the rule. As student pastors, we were born allergic to rules. We love to look for the exceptions, and then use those exceptions as excuses.

We all know some parents with major flaws. But isn't it our tendency to not only exaggerate those flaws, but also evaluate *all* parents with those flaws in mind? We generalize. We label. We disqualify. And it's all based on a perception that may not be entirely fair.

I (Ben) have interacted with a lot of parents. Parents who checked out. Parents who left and never came back. Parents who said some awful things. Parents who hated what I believe. Parents who didn't parent their teenager the way I thought they should (the younger I was, the more I judged).

But honestly, I've never met a parent who genuinely wanted to ruin their kid's life.

I've never met a parent whose main goal was to push their son or daughter in a direction that would lead to hurt, pain, and a critical need for lifelong counseling.

Generally speaking, there are two things that we believe are true about every parent:

 EVERY PARENT WANTS TO BE A GOOD PARENT. EVERY PARENT CAN DO SOMETHING MORE.

What if, instead of focusing on the exceptions to the rule and making excuses to disqualify parents, you focused on those two things?

What if you started acting like you believe in the potential of your students' parents?

Lasting Influence

When I (Ben) was in my first student ministry job, I had a core student who *loved* inviting his friends to our environment. Needless to say, I *loved* that student. One of the many friends he brought to church was a sophomore named Andrew. Within a month, Andrew began dating a girl who attended regularly. I knew he was hooked then!

Andrew had zero church background, but he fully immersed himself in student ministry. He also joined the small group I led. Thanks to my revolutionary leading, Andrew's life started changing dramatically. Okay, it had nothing to do with me—I had no clue what I was doing.

Andrew's parents could care less about church. I went to Andrew's football games and made every effort to connect with them. I didn't invite them to church. I didn't talk about God. I just bragged on their son and told them they had done a great job raising him. Well, that might have been a lie. Yes, I was a student pastor who might have lied to parents. I'm sure you would never do that. Take a minute and pray for me.

Andrew accepted Christ in our student ministry. When it was time for him to get baptized, his parents showed up. By the way, we didn't baptize on Sunday mornings at my church. We baptized in a local lake one day a year. When Andrew's parents arrived, I was ready. I hugged and congratulated them. I said, "Thank you so much for allowing us to play a part in Andrew's life. He's an awesome guy." That wasn't a lie.

One day, Andrew was in a sketch at church on a Sunday morning. His parents showed up! It was a terrible sketch, but they were there. And they met several people who cared *a lot* about Andrew's life.

In the end, Andrew's parents had no interest in church. They did, however, have a lot of interest in Andrew.

Years later, he got married. Here's the crazy part: every groomsman in his wedding had been a part of our original small group. Every. Single. One. To his parents, we were no longer random "church people." We were family. We were a community with names and faces.

Today, Andrew lives eight hours away from me. He lives fifteen minutes away from his parents. I see him twice a year. They see him twice a week. I was highly involved in his life for five or six years. Their involvement has no ending.

 NO MATTER HOW GOOD OF A LEADER YOU ARE, AND NO MATTER WHAT PARENTS OF YOUR STUDENTS ARE LIKE,

THEIR INFLUENCE > **YOUR INFLUENCE.**

Long after student ministry is a distant memory for your students, their parents will be there. **Parents have influence that will far outlast yours.** Your current students will inevitably graduate and move on. Some you'll keep in touch with. Some you won't. Some will become lifelong friends. Some will never return your texts. But you know who will always be in their lives? Their parents. With the exception of a few very rare cases, they will see and communicate with their parents far more than they will communicate with you over the next 50 years.

Your students need you. Their parents need you.

But more than that, your students need their parents.

Speaking "Family"

When we say family, everyone knows what we mean: one mom, one dad, a couple biological children, and a golden retriever. That is, if we're talking about 23% of the U.S. population. For the rest, it looks a little—or a lot—different.

If you've met some of the families of your students, you undoubtedly know that "family" comes in all shapes and sizes. Maybe . . .

> Preston is the oldest of four kids. He spends every day after school looking out for his younger brothers and sisters because his single mom works two jobs to keep up with the bills.

> Kelsey moved out of her house last year to stay with her older sister and boyfriend. She hasn't spoken to her parents since she left.

> Caitlyn lives with her mother and her other mother. She doesn't invite many friends to her house because she isn't she sure what they'd think about her home life. But privately, she loves the two women who love her.

> Cole's mom got remarried last year and decided to start over. At fifteen, he has a little baby sister. Diaper changes are just one of the many pleasant "surprises" in his new reality.

> Sophia's parents were high school sweethearts. She's the oldest of three kids. Her younger brother Asher has down syndrome. She decided in elementary school that she would dedicate her life to helping kids with special needs because of how much she cares for Asher.

You get the point. **Family is a word that means something different to almost every student in your ministry.**

In *Zombies, Football and the Gospel*,[1] Reggie Joiner shares some interesting stats about the landscape of American families today. To gain deeper perspective, you can read the book or examine the latest stats from the U.S. Census Bureau. In the meantime, here are some of the overarching trends the book identified:

More "parents" are . . .
* getting married later
* living together without getting married
* gay and lesbian couples raising children
* single women having children without a male partner to help
* adoptive parents
* mothers of young children who work outside the home
* raising children with special needs
* marrying people of a different race
* living with extended family

This list isn't intended to make a declaration about the state of family in our country. It's meant to simply reveal the trends—trends that you and I should pay attention to. When you *know* that all families are different, it affects how you partner with parents in your student ministry.

It changes how you . . .	1. Connect with families	2. Talk about families from the platform
3. Communicate with families one-on-one	4. Equip families with resources	5. Honor families in conversations with students

The Need To Be Needed

As student pastors, we're a competitive breed of humans. We like being the best, which is a great feature to have. Sometimes, however, that competitiveness fuels a desire in us to be the ultimate leader with the ultimate answers to all of teenage life's ultimate problems. That's extreme, but you get the idea.

The first student I (Ben) ever mentored was a high school junior named Evan. Evan was a cool guy. He played a combination of extreme sports and jock sports, which was rare at that time. He had a great family who loved Jesus. His parents raised him in a healthy home without being overly strict or controlling.

For two years, Evan and I met regularly. It didn't take long for me to notice that he had some issues with his dad.

Like most of you who've been in this profession for a while, I've heard some ugly stories when it comes to fathers and teenage sons. This wasn't one of them. This was a classic dad and 16-year old caught in the crosshairs of freedom, authority, control, and independence. If only all students' problems were like this!

I was 23, and I liked the idea of Evan looking up to me and seeing me as a role model. One day a thought occurred to me: *I wonder if I'm leveraging Evan's complaints about his dad to put myself in the cool chair. Am I letting Evan make his dad the bad authority so I can be the good, go-to authority?*

Once I noticed it, I stopped. And I made a decision that day to **stop pulling students toward me and start pushing students toward parents.**

From that point forward it was easy to push Evan towards his dad. Like I already mentioned, his dad was a solid father. Not perfect, but solid. At 16, Evan had no idea how good he had it compared to most of the teenage world. But it's hard to convince a 16-year old of that. So I simply supported his dad's decisions, tried to look at things from his dad's point of view, and encouraged Evan to show some humility.

Like we said before, all families are different. And certainly not many of them are like Evan's. It's easy to say "Push towards parents" until you hear some of the stories. But for right now, don't focus on them. Think about you. Do you have a nagging need to be needed? Do you have a desire to be viewed as the ultimate authority, even if it's at the expense of parents who—as flawed as they may be—are simply doing the best they can?

More simply, ask yourself this question:

 ARE YOU PUSHING TOWARDS PARENTS OR PULLING TOWARDS YOU?

When you get on stage and speak, are you honoring your students' parents, stepparents, grandparents, or whoever their parental figures may be? Are you showing honor when you hang out with students privately?

It's great for you to be *one* of the go-to authority figures in your students' lives, but make sure you push them in the direction of their families in the process. When you see parents as a bigger influence than you—and push your student ministry *towards* them—you create space for them in your strategy.

We're currently in the process of compiling a list of 50 practical things that student pastors around the country are doing well to partner with parents. There's a lot of great stuff happening out there. But for the sake of time (and our ability to stay up late writing), we're going to give you five ideas.

WHEN YOU MAKE BELIEVE THAT YOU NEED PARENTS, YOU . . .

ONE: CONNECT PARENTS WITH LEADERS

Remember way back in section three when we encouraged you to build a bigger base by developing small group leaders? We challenged you to *not* build student ministry around you. Similarly, we want you to build a bridge with parents. And we want you to do it the same way—through your leaders. After all, if you leave one day, you don't want to take the bridge with you that connects your student ministry to families.

Train your small group leaders to regularly connect with parents.

When you recruit small group leaders, let them know it's an expectation.	When you train small group leaders, cast vision about its importance.	When you meet with small group leaders, hold them accountable to it.

Don't guilt small group leaders. And don't let them exasperate parents. Just keep it simple—encourage them to build a bridge.

Everyone has a different definition of "regularly." As a starting point, push leaders to reach out once a month. It could be a text, phone call, or Facebook message. If you really want to get crazy, encourage handwritten notes and face-to-face meetings. The process isn't as important as the partnership.

To get super-practical, think of it this way:

> **MAKE SURE EVERY PARENT KNOWS THE NAME OF THEIR SON OR DAUGHTER'S SMALL GROUP LEADER.**

It's important for parents to know how much their child's small group leader cares about their family. **Leaders should make it clear that they're not trying to replace parents—they're trying to reinforce them.**

I (Kevin) vividly remember a situation that happened years ago with a high school girl in our ministry. She was struggling in three of her classes. Let's be honest—she was bombing them. When her parents became aware of it, they were not only caught off guard, they were mad. As a parent of teenagers, I can understand.

It didn't take long for a "family meeting" to turn ugly. There they were—dad, mom, and daughter—engaged in a three-way battle. Everybody was blaming everybody.

After 30 intense, frustrating minutes, the daughter abruptly stood up and said, "I need to go call my small group leader." The parents, once again caught off guard, tentatively replied, "Uhh, okay . . ."

The daughter called. The leader answered. With all the dramatic flair that high school girls are known for, the daughter told the leader what was happening. After extending a healthy dose of grace and empathy, the leader turned the tide.

"Your parents have every right to be frustrated. In the end, they're only trying to help you. You may not like the way they're communicating that right now, but that's ultimately what they want."

She continued, "You have the opportunity to make a responsible decision. Since *you're* the one who made the bad grades, let's talk about how *you* can be the one to make this right. We need to come up with a plan."

For some reason, when it came hard truth was received much more open-mindedly coming from the small group leader. The girl walked back into her living room and reengaged with her parents. In a much calmer tone, she explained the situation and then outlined her plan.

For the third time, the parents were caught off guard.

I don't have to tell you whether or not those parents became raving fans of small groups. They saw their daughter's small group leader as an ally, partnering with them to help raise their child in a healthy way.

TWO: CONNECT PARENTS WITH YOUR STRATEGY

You've heard the old saying *seeing is believing*. Sometimes parents need to see your student environment to embrace and support it. One great way to facilitate this is through an event we call Parent Open House.

An open house initiates communication between you, your small group leaders, and the parents of your students. It also gives you a platform to cast vision for your ministry and share your desire to partner with parents to maximize influence in the lives of your students.

A Parent Open House is a great way to . . .

Help your small group leaders connect with parents of students in their group.	Cast vision about your student ministry.	Allow parents to see your environment in action.

Two big questions to answer before you put on this event:

1. What will you do if parents show up?
2. What will you do if they don't?

Let's address the first question. Here are some ways to help leaders connect with parents at this event:

- Set up round tables with small group leaders' names prominently displayed so parents can easily determine where to sit.
- Give leaders and parents time to meet and mingle. Consider providing some icebreaker questions to facilitate discussion.

To help you cast vision . . .

Share your story. Briefly explain how and why you got into student ministry. Just to reiterate, let us again say *briefly*. Preachers love to preach, but this isn't the time to confess the details of your college

Spring Break mistakes. This is the time to let parents know how much you care about what you do.

Share your strategy. Communicate the overarching goal and philosophy of your student ministry. Explain why you do the things you do. Tell parents where you want your program to go, and how you plan on getting there.

Share your goal of partnering with parents. First, make it clear to parents that you don't want to replace them, and neither does their son or daughter's small group leader. Assure parents that *they* are the primary influence in their child's life. Let them know that you aren't trying to give them "parenting advice," especially if you've never been a parent of a teenager. Second, encourage them to widen the circle of influence in their teenager's life so that multiple people are speaking truth into their child's decisions, relationships, thinking, belief, attitude, etc. Third, talk about the importance of the student and small group leader relationship.

To allow parents to see your large group environment in action, simply mark off a specific place where they can observe without being a major distraction. For the sake of maintaining trust and confidentiality in your small groups, allow parents to observe large group only.

If parents *don't* show up, create a simple format for leaders to get a portion of the content to parents. Something as uncomplicated as a one-page Word document will suffice. And here's the key thing to communicate to leaders: **Don't send it to them. Hand it to them.** Let it be an excuse for leaders and parents to meet face-to-face. If there's a zero percent chance of that happening, brainstorm other ways for leaders to distribute that content in a personal way.

[THREE:] CONNECT PARENTS WITH OTHER PARENTS

Like we mentioned in the previous chapter, it's probably a good rule of thumb to *not* tell parents how to parent teenagers, especially if you've never parented one. You can speak as an authority in student culture, but don't speak as an authority in parenting.

Instead, **allow parents to learn from other parents.** There are a lot of ways you can do this, but one simple way is creating a parent Facebook page for your student ministry.

Find a parent who . . .

has already raised a teenager or two	is gracious and self-aware	has the time and ability to effectively monitor the page

. . .and empower him or her to spearhead this endeavor.

Encourage them to lead with humility and not act like they have it all figured out. It's a great way for parents to network, share tips and struggles, and stay connected to your vision and strategy. One of the best things that could emerge from this is parents meeting for coffee and helping each other win . . . or at least, survive.

Let your Facebook group leader know which topics you're currently discussing in student ministry. Your content will hopefully give them a head start when it comes to creating discussion points online.

If they don't talk parenting, they can always use the Facebook page to sell stuff to each other and recommend good plumbers and dentists.

FOUR: CONNECT PARENTS WITH THEIR KIDS

One of the things we provide in *XP3 Students* curriculum is a series-based email to parents. It's called the Parent CUE, and we've defined it as "Parent-specific Intel that gets mom and dad off the bleachers and in the game."

After a short description of our current series, we include content that we hope will educate and encourage parents in areas that are relevant to their relationship with their kids. Nothing overwhelming—excerpts from articles or blog posts that could potentially lead to parents thinking things like, *Oh, wow, I'm so glad I learned that about the teenage brain.*

Finally, we challenge them to take one step. Here are some examples of things we've encouraged parents to do:

- Invite your teenage son or daughter to help you figure out one thing you could do to help an elderly neighbor or single mom. It could be as simple as making (or buying) them dinner and delivering it to their house.
- During one meal this week, put away all social media and brainstorm 3-4 words that you'd like to describe your family.
- Identify one creative way you can show love and acceptance to your son or daughter this week.
- Share a story of what it was like growing up where you lived as a teenager. Was it a big city or a small town? Was there a lot going on, or were you often bored? How did your hometown shape who you are today?
- Ask your teenager for ideas on something they think would be fun to do as a family. Students tend to engage more when they have input.

We try hard not to bombard them. Not all parents are ready for God/Church/Bible stuff. Like we've already mentioned, some of them have zero respect for—or interest in—faith. So we don't email and ask them to pray out loud or lead family devotions. Those things are awesome, we've just realized that it would make some parents hyperventilate out of fear or intimidation (and, they would delete every email we send from that point forward). Instead, we focus on topics like conflict and priorities in hopes that it could lead to discussions about faith later.

One other way we do this is by providing a family series each year. We pinpoint topics that are relevant to families, particularly to the parent-teenager relationship. For example, XP3 Students released a series called *The Fighter*, where we encouraged students to fight *for* their relationship with their parents instead of just fighting to get what they want. Similarly, we encouraged parents to fight *for* their relationship with their teenager instead of just fighting to control the situation. Series like this provide a great opportunity for you to encourage parents to invest time *now* in the relationship they want to have with their son or daughter *later*.

FIVE: CONNECT PARENTS WITH BIG MOMENTS

Big moments create big opportunities for you to connect with parents. Baptism is a perfect example.

I (Kevin) don't like it when students get baptized on mission trips or at summer camps. Don't get me wrong. I *love* the idea of them getting baptized. I just dislike the idea of their parents being left out of the experience.

So here's a practical step: **don't do that.** Like we said earlier in this book, you probably don't like being told what to do or what not to do. Here's the good news—I'm not your boss. The choice is yours. But I encourage you to at least give parents, stepparents, and grandparents the chance to show up. When you're in Mexico, they have no chance.

I can think of several times when student baptisms opened the door for parents and stepparents to come to church for the first time. Some of them never came back. But some of them did. It gave me an opportunity to meet them. It gave their son or daughter's small group leader a chance to interact with them face-to-face. And church became relationships and people instead of rules and traditions.

Some of you have been baptizing on trips for years. We understand. By no means are we trying to downplay or discredit what has already happened. Just the fact that you *take* students to events where they can have life-changing experiences is awesome. One time we determined that of our students who put their trust in Christ for the first time, over 90 percent of them pointed back to a camp, retreat, or mission trip as the moment when it clicked.

But when those life-changing experiences open the door for another life-changing experience—baptism—we think you should make it possible for parents to see it in person.

BIG MOMENTS CREATE BIG OPPORTUNITIES FOR YOU TO CONNECT WITH PARENTS

Time for a good old fashioned mad lib. Fill out this list:

1. ADJECTIVE: ....

2. NAME: ....

3. VERB: ....

4. NOUN: ....

5. VERB: ....

6. VERB: ....

7. ADJECTIVE: ....

8. ADVERB: ....

NOW WRITE IN YOUR ANSWERS, IN ORDER:

Once there was a .... student in your ministry
(ADJECTIVE)

named .... He had trouble with his parents
(NAME)

because they'd always .... at his
(VERB)

.... But you helped the family by telling
(NOUN)

them to .... and ....
(VERB)   (VERB)

Everybody was .... and lived
(ADJECTIVE)

.... ever after.
(ADVERB)

Now that you have that specific family situation figured out, it's time
to take a step towards parents in general. Write down one way you
can encourage your leaders to connect with parents this week:

IT STARTS WITH YOU

The Next Generation

At this point, we've exhausted the five ideas that we want you to imagine. And we've proposed *a lot* of behaviors that we think will reinforce those ideas. Now the question is, "Will you make yourself believe them?"

- **Make yourself believe that you'll be here forever.** See student ministry as the most important job in the world. And while you're there, work on making it great.

- **Make yourself believe that you'll leave one day.** Invest in leaders that can sustain the ministry long after you leave. And build a foundation that can effectively reach more students in a healthy way.

- **Make yourself believe that your senior pastor's right.** Follow now, so that you will be more equipped to lead later. And instead of criticizing your senior pastor, learn from them.

- **Make yourself believe that your children's pastor is cool.** View their job as vital. And experience the benefits of working with them to accomplish a greater strategy.

- **Make yourself believe that parents matter.** Envision a greater potential in the parents of your students. And encourage the relationships that will be standing long after students leave your ministry.

We believe that these five ideas will not only strengthen your student ministry, they will bring more peace into your life. This is a healthier way of approaching a job that is notoriously unhealthy. It's better for your family. It's better for your future. And it's better for your faith.

Margin. Rest. Confidence. Creativity. Just a few of the payoffs when you make believe.

The next generation needs . . .

student pastors who will stick around for a while.
small group leaders who will be present in their life.
churches that have a unified staff.
children's ministries where students can serve in.
parents who are empowered for the long haul.

But it all starts with you.

And your imagination.

Works Cited

Part One: Head in the Clouds
[1] InspirationalStories.com. <http://www.inspirationalstories.com/quotes/nelson-mandela-the-power-of-imagination-created-the-illusion/>

[2] Mathew 28:19, NIV

[3] Matthew 28:20, NIV

[4] 2 Peter 1:1, NIV

Part One: Catalysts for Change
[5] Romans 12:2, NIV

Part Two: The Most Important Job in the World
[1] Senior, Jennifer. "Why You Never Truly Leave High School." *New York Magazine*. 20 Jan. 2013. <http://nymag.com/news/features/high-school-2013-1/>

[2] American Psychological Association. "Are Teens Adopting Adults' Stress Habits?" *Stress in America*. 14 Feb. 2011. <https://www.apa.org/news/press/releases/stress/2013/stress-report.pdf>

[3] Center for Disease Control and Prevention. "Suicide Prevention." <http://www.cdc.gov/violenceprevention/pub/youth_suicide.html>

[4] Lachman, Robert. "More Teens Cutting Themselves Today." *Hudson Valley Parent*. <http://www.hvparent.com/health-report-tween-cutting>

[5] National Association of African American Studies & Affiliates. "Bullying Statistics/Cyber-Bullying Statistics/School Bullying Statistics." <http://naaas.org/statistics.pdf>

Part Two: Reverse the Turnover Rate
[6] Youth Ministry Institute. <http://yminstitute.com/about/history/>

Part Three: You'll Leave One Day
[1] Business Mastering.com <http://www.businessmastering.com/en.html#quotes>

Part Five: The Importance of Childhood
[1] Lee, R. S. *Your Growing Child and Religion*. Penguin Books, 1967.

Part Five: Work On Something Together
[2] Reyes, Julian. "Iraqi and Utah students work together to close culture gaps." Deseret News. 10 Jul. 2012. <http://www.deseretnews.com/article/865558840/Iraqi-and-Utah-students-work-together-to-close-culture-gaps.html?pg=all>

About the Authors

Ben Crawshaw leads the student initiative (*XP3 Students* & *High School Camp*) at Orange. At 19, Ben began traveling and speaking to students. He graduated from Lee University in Cleveland, TN, and then took a job as an assistant pastor at age 22. After that, Ben became the Creative Director of High School Ministry at North Point Community Church, where he produced programs, media, and events for over 2,000 students. He currently writes, speaks, hosts and creates camps for students all over the United States (and a couple of other countries, too). In his free time, you can find Ben doing the Braves' Tomahawk Chop, watching non-horror movies, or eating Reese's Pieces. He and his wife Holly love living in Dahlonega, GA. They have two daughters and an unruly cat named Cupcake. Learn more about Ben at bencrawshaw.org.

Kevin Ragsdale serves on the Leadership Team for North Point Ministries and is the Multi-Campus High School Director of North Point Community Church and its four other Atlanta-area campuses. Kevin was one of the first family ministry employees at North Point and developed their student ministry philosophy, which includes the small-group model. He also created Student Impact, a program that provides an opportunity for students to serve every week in the church. In addition to leading a staff on that is responsible for over 2,000 high school students every week, Kevin also designs environments, oversees curriculum, roots for the Oklahoma Sooners, and plays hypercompetitive pickup basketball. Kevin and his wife Gina live in Cumming, Georgia, with their three children.